Summer End

A Play

Eric Chappell

A SAMUEL FRENCH ACTING EDITION

FOUNDED 1830

SAMUELFRENCH-LONDON.CO.UK
SAMUELFRENCH.COM

ISBN 978-0-573-01995-1

www.samuelfrench-london.co.uk

www.samuelfrench.com

FOR AMATEUR PRODUCTION ENQUIRIES

UNITED KINGDOM AND WORLD
EXCLUDING NORTH AMERICA
plays@SamuelFrench-London.co.uk
020 7255 4302/01

Each title is subject to availability from Samuel French,

depending upon country of performance.

SUMMER END

First presented at the Lane Theatre, Newquay, in August 2002, with the following cast:

Emily Baines	Ann Capel
May Brewer	Jean Lenton
Sally	Simmone Bundy/Ginnie McPherson
Mrs Lang	Pam Heywood
Alan Baines	Gerry Shipp

Directed by Mary Downie

CHARACTERS

Emily Baines, late seventies-early eighties
May Brewer, late seventies
Sally, a carer, about thirty
Mrs Lang, retirement home supervisor, late forties
Alan Baines, Emily's son, fifties

The action of the play takes place in the room shared by Emily Baines and May Brewer in the Summer End retirement home

Time — the present

SYNOPSIS OF SCENES

ACT I

Scene 1 A Sunday evening in late November
Scene 2 Early evening a few days before Christmas

ACT II

Two hours later

Also by Eric Chappell
published by Samuel French Ltd

Double Vision
Fiddlers Three (We Don't Want to Lose You *and* Cut and Dried)
Haunted
Haywire
Heatstroke (Snakes and Ladders)
It Can Damage Your Health
Natural Causes
Something's Burning
Theft
Up and Coming

ACT I

SCENE 1

A bedsitting-room at the Summer End retirement home. A Sunday evening in late November

Please refer to the set plan on p. 60

The bedsitting-room is L-shaped with another room — the bathroom — taking up the UL corner. A door links the two rooms. The main door into the room is DR; a glass-panelled door DL, which is incorporated into a window, leads to a fire-escape. There is another window UC. There are two single beds in the room, one (Emily's) UR next to the window, one DL (May's) with its head against the bathroom wall; both have bell-cords, and bedside tables with drawers. Each table has a lamp and decanter of water on it; there is a music box on Emily's table, a handbag on May's. There is a wardrobe against the wall DL, next to the fire door. Near this door is a hook for the key — but the key is missing

There is a shared area DR where personal items of furniture mingle with the furniture of the home. There are two easy chairs with cushions, an occasional table and a large, old-fashioned dresser/cupboard covered in bric-a-brac which stands by the wall. A wheelchair stands in the corner

When the play begins, Emily Baines and May Brewer are sitting in the two easy chairs by the occasional table. There are two teacups on the table

May is reading the local paper. She is in her late seventies. She is a small, fussily-dressed woman with an obvious desire to please. She is still quite sprightly, colours her hair and wears make-up. Emily, in contrast, is firmly rooted in her chair. She is older than May and her white hair is set in a defiant perm; nevertheless her skin is smooth and her expression alert. Her trademark is an eloquent sniff to show disbelief or disdain

May It's not in.
Emily Not even in the announcements?
May No.
Emily (*with grim satisfaction*) What did I tell you? Ignored. Well, it doesn't surprise me. Not with the state of things here.
May Annie Robbins is in.
Emily Annie Robbins?

May Ninety-six.

Emily She never was.

May (*reading*) Ninety-six ... Originally of Artichoke Yard.

Emily (*incredulously*) Artichoke Yard?

May Yes.

Emily They came out of Paradise Place.

May That's not mentioned here. The family obviously prefer to be associated with Artichoke Yard.

Emily I'm not surprised — the sanitation in Paradise Place left a lot to be desired.

May It says she had an active mind ——

Emily (*more surprised*) Active! Annie Robbins?

May — right to the end.

Emily She never had an active mind — not even at the beginning.

May And she had many tales to tell.

Emily Yes, and one of them was that she was ninety-six. If she was ninety-six how could she have been at school with our Win?

May I don't know.

Emily Our Win would have been eighty-six if the good Lord had spared her — and they were in the same class at school. You're good at arithmetic, May. If she was ten years older than our Win when they left school — how old would she have been?

May (*considering*) Twenty-four.

Emily Her mind couldn't have been that active then, could it?

May I'm merely reading what it says here, Emily. It's probably a misprint.

Emily Does it mention the time she was a presser at the steam laundry?

May (*consulting the paper*) No.

Emily No, I thought they'd draw a veil over that.

May It says she was a keen gardener and had green fingers.

Emily Not in Artichoke Yard. Nothing grew there.

May What about artichokes?

Emily I never saw any.

May They called it Artichoke Yard.

Emily They called it Paradise Place but it wasn't paradise — not with four families to a lav. (*Pause*) So she's not in.

May (*searching in the paper*) What was her name again?

Emily (*sighing*) Bella. Bella Bottomley. Don't tell me you've forgotten her already.

May I didn't know her very well.

Emily The least you could do is remember her name. You're sitting in her chair.

May (*wincing*) Don't, Emily.

Emily Don't worry — she didn't die in it. (*She gives a macabre nod*) She died in the bed.

May You know I don't like to think about it. (*She puts the paper down*) Perhaps she'll be in next week.

Emily She won't be in.

May Why not?

Emily Because they don't want it in.

May Who's they?

Emily The powers that be. They want to keep it quiet.

May Why should they want to keep it quiet?

Emily You haven't been here long enough. You don't know the workings. They don't want it to get out.

May Why not? The poor soul died — that's all.

Emily No, that's not all, May.

May What do you mean?

Emily (*glancing at the door and lowering her voice*) Suppose I was to tell you that Bella shouldn't have died — that it wasn't a natural death ...

May (*staring*) You mean, she died of neglect?

Emily No. I'm dying of neglect. She died of something worse...

May (*leaning forward, thoroughly intrigued*) Then what was it?

Emily (*smiling mysteriously*) I can't tell you that. I've told enough already.

May You haven't told me anything.

Emily I keep my own counsel. And when you've been here a bit longer you'll learn to do the same.

May Well, I like it here.

Emily I don't. And if I had the use of my legs I'd be out of here like a shot. This place gives me the creeps. Do you know what it reminds me of?

May What?

Emily A house in one of those films ...

May What films?

Emily Where they all sit around talking quite happily until half-way through the evening they find out they're dead.

May Really, Emily! It's nothing like that. Everyone's so nice and friendly.

Emily They are to your face.

May And it's a lovely room.

Emily Of course it's a lovely room. It was intended for the staff — until they moved them out.

May Why did they move them out?

Emily For the money. They wanted to make room for a few more bodies. They'll be stepping over us soon. Lord help us if there's a fire. We'll be burnt to a crisp.

May (*nodding*) At least we're next to the emergency exit.

Emily Emergency exit! The emergency will be when they try to find the key — it's been missing for weeks. We'll be knotting sheets, mark my words. No wonder tempers are short.

May I haven't noticed. Everyone's so helpful. Nothing's too much trouble. Clean knickers every day. You only have to drop a garment to the floor and it's away and washed.

Emily But does it come back?

May They should have name tags in them, Emily.

Emily They do have name tags but the ink gets washed off and then they're anybody's. It'll happen to yours.

May I don't think so. I won't be here long enough.

Emily (*doubtfully*) Won't you?

May Not once Frank's made the necessary arrangements.

Emily What arrangements?

May He's having plans drawn up for a Granny flat.

Emily (*unimpressed*) Granny flat. They put our Win in one of those. Looked more like a clothes closet to me. I think that's what finished her in the end — claustrophobia.

May I'm sure it'll be nothing like a clothes closet.

Emily (*with a sly grin*) Well, when you move in, look around for the clothes closet; if you can't find one, you're in it.

May No — this will be a proper extension.

Emily That'll take time.

May I could have gone up earlier but Frank wanted to be sure I could stand the upheaval.

Emily Upheaval? It's only Scotland. I don't call that an upheaval. You're not going to walk it, are you?

May My heart's not strong. That's why Frank wanted me to come in here for a while — for the rest.

Emily You won't get any rest here. They pull you out of bed too early for that. But while you are here, let me give you some advice. Don't take your rings off.

May I never remove my rings.

Emily That was my mistake.

May Is it still missing?

Emily Along with a gold crucifix.

May They say opals are unlucky.

Emily It was for me.

May Opals means tears.

Emily Well, I've shed plenty of those since I've been here.

May regards Emily thoughtfully

May Funny how these things always happen to you, Emily.

Emily I'm not the only one. Bella's sapphire went missing after she died.

May Are you sure?

Emily They were looking high and low for it.

May I remember it — it was a lovely ring. Although I've always preferred diamonds myself. (*She looks at her fingers approvingly*)

Emily So I've noticed.

May Harry was always very generous.

Emily Well, anyone who'd kept a fish and chip shop for thirty years could afford to be — they're gold mines.

May Well, it was more of a cafeteria towards the end. We'd moved into pies, chicken nibbles and kebabs — and we were serving wine. We were even contemplating vegetarian — when it happened ... (*She falters*)

Emily I heard he collapsed in the fryer.

May No, he didn't. But it was sudden. We'd been planning to go up the Suez Canal that summer.

Emily Good thing you didn't. He'd have only collapsed there. Then you'd have had to get him back. That would have meant a mountain of paperwork.

May We should have retired. If only we'd known.

Emily You never know what's round the corner, May, but you can depend on one thing — it's usually unpleasant.

The door bursts open and Sally, a carer, enters carrying a tray. She is about thirty and heavily made up. She has a slightly sulky manner, mainly directed towards Emily. There's clearly no love between them

Emily sniffs

What did I tell you?

Sally bangs her tray down on the table

Sally Finished with your cups?

May (*ingratiatingly*) Yes. Have you, Emily?

Emily maintains a bleak silence. May helps Sally to assemble the tea things during the following

Going off soon, Sally?

Sally Not soon enough. I've been on my feet all day.

Emily (*to no-one in particular*) I wish I could have been on my feet all day — I wouldn't complain. Some people should try a wheelchair.

Sally darts Emily a glance but ignores the remark

May (*hurriedly*) How are the wedding plans coming along, Sally?

Sally He's getting cold feet again.

May He's not.
Sally He says he's too young to get tied down. He's thirty-five.

Emily sniffs disparagingly

Sally Do you know what he said last night? He said it's like yoking a wild
   stallion to the plough.
May He never did.
Sally He did. I said it's a bit late to start talking like that — I've ordered the
   dress.
May Oh, what's it like, Sally?
Sally (*thawing*) Ivory silk brocade — Venetian style with deep sleeves.
May You'll look a picture, Sally. Won't she, Emily?

Another sniff from Emily

Sally If I get there. It's not as if he hasn't seen something of life. Do you know
   what he's doing this week? Destroying his old love letters. Hundreds of
   them. I thought they'd have to take them away in a skip.
May Well, at least he's experienced, Sally. I think it's better to marry
   someone experienced.
Sally He's already complained about the expense.
May He's not.
Sally He has. I wouldn't mind but he's only paying for two taxis. He expects
   everyone else to find their own way.
May Hasn't he offered to help with the rest?
Sally No; he says it's tradition for the bride's father to pay for the rest — and
   he doesn't want to break with tradition. I told him, my father doesn't mind
   breaking with tradition — he's leaving it to me.
May I don't know how you do it, Sally.

Sally draws the curtains during the following

Sally And you should see his guest list. He hasn't stinted there. Twenty-four
   people from East Kilbride. I said I was hoping for a quiet wedding — not
   much chance of that with twenty-four people from East Kilbride. He said
   they usually bring a haggis. I said that'll go a long way. And he's got
   another sixteen coming from Dunton Basset. I didn't know there were
   sixteen people in Dunton Basset! And I've been trying to cut costs to the
   bone. We've already compromised on a cold ham salad with a fruit cocktail
   starter — and then we're going way over budget. And the only presents to
   arrive from East Kilbride so far are a pair of oven gloves, a bread board and
   a plastic bucket. I said to Ian, we won't get our fitted kitchen that way.

May That reminds me, Sally. Could we have sight of the present list? Emily and I would like to make a contribution.

Emily looks at May in surprise

Sally I've got it here. (*She takes the list from her pocket and hands it to May*) Don't rush. Last night he said had I thought about being a common-law wife. I told him — there's nothing common about me.

Sally exits with the tea things

Emily Who does she think she's kidding?

May Do you want to see the list?

Emily I don't hold with lists.

May It avoids duplication; they cross things off as they're bought. My! (*Reading*) Fridge-freezer … Tumble-dryer … Eye-level grill …

Emily Well, they're a few things that won't get crossed off — not with that lot. Eye-level grill … One thing's certain: she won't be cooking eye-level food — that family's always lived out of tins.

May Well, we don't have to buy things like that.

Emily I'm not buying anything. (*Darkly*) You notice she never spoke to me.

May You never spoke to her.

Emily It's her place to speak to me.

May Not after you reported her. She was bound to be upset.

Emily If she can't stand criticism.

May You said she'd tried to drown you in the bath.

Emily She did. I had to fight for my life. I've never been so roughly handled. I was going down for the third time when Mrs Lang came in. Sally's always had it in for me. She was all over Bella — far too friendly. But she didn't fool me. She was only after what she could get.

May Emily!

Emily You watch out for her, May. You'll be next. Do you know how she can afford this wedding? Scrounging. She eats for nothing — and not just when she's here; when she leaves that carrier bag's bulging. No wonder food's scarce.

May (*rising*) I must say for someone with glaucoma you don't miss much. Well, I'm not going to listen to any more tittle-tattle. I have to get ready.

Emily Aren't you going to read the rest of the funerals?

May No — I'm going to the service. (*She takes a bottle of scent from her handbag and dabs some behind her ears*)

Emily Does that require scent?

May I like to smell nice. (*Pointedly*) We all need to take more care as we get older, Emily. That's why we should take our baths regularly and so forth… People don't always tell you when you smell.

Emily Don't worry — I'll tell you. (*She watches May's preparations with interest*) And will Vernon Watts be at the service?

May I've no idea.

Emily He's been going very regularly since you came.

May He's a born-again Christian.

Emily (*shocked*) He never is.

May He is.

Emily Vernon Watts?

May Totally immersed.

Emily He never was.

May In a bath specially hired for the occasion — to wash away all his sins.

Emily Must have been a big bath.

May Then he confessed them to the congregation.

Emily I wish I'd been there. (*Pause*) Did he mention Bella Bottomley?

May I've no idea. I wasn't present. But if you're suggesting he sinned with Bella Bottomley ——

Emily I'm not suggesting anything but I know what I know...

May Emily, I won't hear a word against Vernon. He's been a tower of strength to me since I came here.

Emily He was a tower of strength to Bella Bottomley and where did it get her? Dead.

May Do I detect a note of jealousy?

Emily Jealous!

May After all, Vernon is the most presentable man at Summer End.

Emily What do you mean the most? He's the only presentable man at Summer End. And that's not saying much. But handsome is as handsome does, May Brewer.

May He does have this lovely smile.

Emily He's not smiling — he's baring his teeth. You should be careful at your age.

May My age? Do you know what Mrs Lang said to me the other day? (*Pointedly*) She said some people can't wait to grow old — they rush to meet it. She says she could never be like that. That's why she's on that three letter thing.

Emily What three letter thing?

May It's a course of treatment — with hormones.

Emily What's it supposed to do?

May Keep her young.

Emily It's not working.

May Actually it's very effective.

Emily continues to watch May's preparations

Emily You're not on it, are you?

May No!

Emily I just wondered. Well, remember age has its advantages. As your looks fade — so does his eyesight.

May There's nothing wrong with his eyesight. (*She opens the drawer of her bedside table, takes out her purse and prayer book and puts them on the table. Pause*) Should I ask them to fetch you?

Emily No, I'm not going. Our Alan's here. He's in with Lang. They're having a meeting.

May What about?

Emily (*indignantly*) About me. I'm under discussion. (*Proudly*) And not for the first time. They had a meeting about me last week. There were four of them — and two in attendance.

May Six of them! What do they find to talk about?

Emily The question is: can I cope?

May I should have thought the question was can they cope.

Emily It's the same thing. Is my incapacity temporary or permanent.

May It seems pretty permanent to me.

Emily Do I need nursing care. That's what has to be decided.

May Do you need nursing care? You're getting it already. You had me up three times last night.

Emily I'm sorry. If I had the use of my legs I wouldn't dream of disturbing you. What am I supposed to do — wet myself?

May You're supposed to press your bell.

Emily It doesn't work.

May Of course it works.

Emily Then why don't they come?

May Because you don't press it.

Emily They don't come because I'm out of favour. I know too much about this place — that's why they want me out.

May The way you're going they'll have you out. (*She picks up her prayer book and purse*)

Emily At least I'll leave here upright — not like poor Bella. (*Quickly*) Before you go — help me through, would you?

May Ring the bell.

Emily I haven't time for that.

May sighs, helps Emily into her wheelchair and pushes her towards the bathroom

May I'm not staying. Frankly, I'm getting fed up with the sight of your bottom.

Emily Well, if you can't help a body. Is it too much to ask? Why do you think you were put in here?

May Because Mrs Turner was sick and needed attention — that's why I was put in here.

Emily It was not. It was because I was sick and needed attention. That's why they chose someone able-bodied — to give me a helping hand.

May Well, I won't be able-bodied for long. I'll probably go the same way as Bella.

Emily grips May's arm fiercely

Emily What's that supposed to mean?

May Emily, you're hurting my arm.

Emily Bella's death was nothing to do with me.

May I didn't say it was.

Emily That's all right then ... (*She relaxes her grip*)

They proceed into the bathroom

(*Off; grumbling*) I don't know who converted this place but he must have been out of his mind. You can't swing a cat round. Summer End. Well, they certainly got the name right. I haven't been warm since I got here.

During the following, May returns from the bathroom, leaving the door half-open, and presses the switch on Emily's bell-cord. She hesitates for a moment, then crosses to her bedside table. She takes a small bottle of sherry from the drawer and takes a furtive nip, then returns it

May hurries from the room by the main door, forgetting her purse and prayer book

Mrs Lang enters with Emily's son Alan. Mrs Lang is an elegant woman in her late forties. Alan Baines is in his fifties. He is wearing an untidy raincoat and looks harassed

Alan's expression becomes more miserable as he listens to his mother. Mrs Lang's smile becomes slightly fixed

(*Off*) Still, things will warm up when those Christmas decorations catch fire. They'd never pass inspection. Then what would we do. Some are three to a room — they'd be wedged in the doorway. And what about me? That lift only takes one — that doesn't conform to regulations. They put me in, press the button, then dash downstairs to meet me. If they're waylaid I'm up and down like a yo-yo. I arrive in that dining-room like a cold rice pudding — and my stomach's still on the top floor...

Mrs Lang closes the bathroom door gently and makes to speak

Sally bursts into the room

Sally Did she ring?

Mrs Lang I shouldn't think so, Sally. Mrs Baines won't touch anything that may have wires attached to it — unfortunately. Don't worry — I'll see to her.

Sally backs uncertainly towards the door

Oh, and, Sally — don't forget to knock in the future. This is Mrs Baines' home and we should treat it as such.

Sally (*sulkily*) She gets impatient.

Mrs Lang Mrs Baines may get impatient but that's the privilege of the elderly — after all, they haven't as much time as we have, have they, Sally?

Sally No, Mrs Lang.

Sally hesitates

Mrs Lang Thank you, Sally.

Sally exits with bad grace

(*Sighing*) Such a lumpish girl. She has no more idea how to leave a room than she has how to enter it. Although I'm afraid she's been more difficult since your mother reported her.

Alan Oh, is that the one?

Mrs Lang Yes.

Alan (*lightly*) Mother said she tried to drown her.

Mrs Lang (*smiling*) I don't think it was that serious. Sally can be rather clumsy and her mind is on other things but then your mother doesn't like baths. I think they were evenly matched. When I arrived, drawn by the shouts, Sally was a good deal wetter than your mother. And afterwards she showed me her bruises.

Alan Bruises?

Mrs Lang Your mother may have no strength in her legs but she has a powerful grip. I suppose it's having to take the weight on her arms ... Actually, we didn't realize she was quite so incapacitated when we accepted her.

Alan (*uneasily*) She does have her good days.

Mrs Lang Does she? We did agree on a trial period to see if she'd settle in — but I'm afraid she hasn't. Don't think it's because she's become

enfeebled. (*She checks that the bathroom door is firmly closed*) Many of
our residents are that — although she may need more dedicated nursing
than we can provide. No, it's when they become disruptive that we have
a problem. (*She checks the room for tidiness and dust during the following*)

Alan Has she become disruptive?

Mrs Lang She won't press her bell. She insists upon banging the floor with
her stick in the middle of the night. Unfortunately we're just above the rest
room and old Mrs James has yet to enjoy a peaceful night. She points out
with some justification if it's a rest room why isn't she getting any rest?

Alan I'll have a word with Mother.

Mrs Lang Don't misunderstand me. I'm fond of your mother. She's a
character — but she does have a stubborn streak. And if she's not happy
here ...

Alan Mrs Lang, she wouldn't be happy anywhere.

Mrs Lang It's not as if we can't deal with difficult old ladies. That's not the
problem. It's her effect on the other residents. I'm afraid she's caused many
a sleepless night. She's the only one here who claims to have seen a
prowler.

Alan Has there been a prowler?

Mrs Lang There has according to Emily. She says she's seen him on the fire
escape in the middle of the night.

Alan Do you think that's possible?

Mrs Lang Since Emily's almost bedridden, suffers from glaucoma and the
fire escape is not in her line of vision, I should think it's most unlikely.

Alan So you think she's beginning to imagine things?

Mrs Lang (*lowering her voice*) There has been some deterioration since she
came here. Memory loss, delusions — and the doctor has detected some
signs of approaching senility.

Alan Oh, no.

Mrs Lang But that's our worry. What I'd like you to deal with is her
obsession with Bella Bottomley.

Alan What obsession? She hasn't said anything to me.

Mrs Lang She believes that Bella didn't die from natural causes and that Mr
Watts is somehow implicated.

Alan Why should she think that?

Mrs Lang Vernon Watts was rather fond of Bella — very attentive. I think
your mother may have been jealous — although why she should suspect
him ... Unless...

Alan Unless what?

Mrs Lang (*after a pause*) Well, when we found Bella, there were some
contusions about the face. Emily may have heard the doctor discussing it
with me. He felt Bella may have fallen shortly before she died. And then
there was a ring that went missing, a sapphire. Your mother believes
Vernon took it.

Alan My God! (*He pauses*) Doesn't she say some of her things have gone missing too?

Mrs Lang Yes, an opal ring and a crucifix. But I don't take too much notice of that. They're probably in her dresser. She's becoming very forgetful.

Alan Have you looked?

Mrs Lang Oh, no. That's Emily's private property ...

Alan approaches the cupboard to start a search

But if you could persuade her to look — it would avoid suspicion falling on others.

Alan (*turning back from the cupboard*) I will have a word with her, Mrs Lang.

Mrs Lang puts a finger to her lips. She opens the bathroom door and exits

Alan tries the cupboard door and finds it locked during the following

Mrs Lang (*off*) You have done well, Emily. You've managed all by yourself. Alan's come to see you.

Emily (*off*) What does he want?

Mrs Lang (*off*) He's come for a chat.

Emily (*off*) He'll want something...

Mrs Lang reappears with Emily in her wheelchair

Mrs Lang and Alan assist Emily into her easy chair. She regards them suspiciously

Mrs Lang Now I'm going to get you a nice cup of tea while you have a chat ...

Mrs Lang exits with the wheelchair

Alan (*brightly*) Well, how are you, Mother?

Emily Don't shout.

Alan I'm not shouting.

Emily Everyone shouts. Keep your voice down. She'll hear you.

Alan Mrs Lang's gone for the tea.

Emily Tea! They don't know how to make it. I haven't had a decent cup since I've been here. It's dishwater.

Alan You have to take the rough with the smooth, Mother.

Emily I've had the rough; when am I going to get the smooth, that's what I want to know. (*Pause*) What did she say about me?

Alan You should ring the bell.

Emily I'll give her ring the bell.

Alan You disturbed Mrs James last night and she's not well.

Emily If she's not well they should put her in the rest room.

Alan She is in the rest room, it's below here.

Emily (*staring*) It never is.

Alan It is.

Emily Well, how's that for planning? Putting it below here.

Alan When they put it there they didn't know someone was going to go mad with a walking stick in the middle of the night. (*He opens a drawer to search through it*)

Emily (*sharply*) What are you doing?

Alan I'm looking for the key to the cupboard.

Emily Why?

Alan I'm looking for that opal ring of yours. People are falling under suspicion.

Emily Are they?

Alan Don't worry, I don't want to see your savings book.

Emily You're not going to.

Alan You'll have to declare it one day.

Emily That's for my old age.

Alan You've reached it. (*He lowers his voice*) You're being subsidized by the state, Mother. If you don't spend it, the government's going to take it from you.

Emily If you don't get there first.

Alan Don't start that again. For the last time, I don't want anything that belongs to you.

Emily Then what's happened to my green and gold wicker linen basket?

Alan (*staring*) What? (*Pause*) It's in my garage.

Emily And the dressing-table with the oval mirror?

Alan That's in the garage.

Emily And the marble washstand?

Alan The same.

Emily (*suspiciously*) All in the garage. I'm surprised there's room for the car.

Alan There isn't. That stands outside.

Emily Along with my three-piece suite I suppose.

Alan No — that's gone.

Emily (*aghast*) Gone! Gone where?

Alan (*uneasily*) We got rid of it.

Emily What! You mean I'm without a three-piece suite?

Alan You're not coming back, Mother. The council wanted the flat. We couldn't keep paying rent. And there was no more room in the garage.

Emily (*after a pause*) How much did you get for it?

Alan Nothing.

Emily Nothing! A suite in quilted leather with moquette cushions? Nothing!

Alan No-one wanted it.

Emily No-one wanted a three-piece leather suite!

Alan It wasn't leather, it was simulated — and it was badly worn.

Emily It never was.

Alan It was. I had to pay them ten pounds to take it away.

Emily Take it away? Take it where?

Alan To the tip.

Emily (*appalled*) You mean you sent a three-piece suite in quilted leather with moquette cushions to the tip? You must be mad. Not that it would have got there: once they were round the corner it would have been off-loaded — probably already had a customer for it.

Alan Mother, your stuff's out of date — and they're not collectors' items. Sotheby's aren't waiting for the arrival of your three-piece suite — or your marble washstand.

Emily You're so sharp you'll cut yourself. (*Bitterly*) My things may not mean much to you but they were all I had ... (*She almost falters for a moment*)

Alan (*patting her sympathetically*) I know. I'd have kept everything if I could. I just didn't have the room. (*Pause*) Now where's the key to the cupboard?

Emily It's lost.

Alan Where did you see it last?

Emily (*slowly*) It was in a piece of tissue paper — together with my little scissors — and my cotton wool.

Alan (*patiently*) And do you remember where you put the little scissors and the cotton wool?

Emily (*staring*) In the tissue paper.

Alan (*sighing*) I know that, but where did you put the tissue paper?

Emily In the blue purse.

Alan Now we're getting somewhere. And where's the blue purse?

Emily In the cupboard.

Alan Good. (*He approaches the cupboard and stops*) But the cupboard's locked!

Emily Well, that's it then.

Alan That's not it! The key can't be in the blue purse with the tissue paper, the scissors and the cotton wool because the cupboard's locked!

Emily Don't shout.

Alan I'm not shouting. (*He pauses for a moment and looks round the room*) I know where you used to keep it ... In the music box.

Emily What music box?

Alan The one on your bedside table. The one Dad bought. You kept the key in there so you could always hear if one of us lifted the lid ... (*He crosses to the bedside table*)

Emily It doesn't play any more.

Alan lifts the lid of the box and the music begins to play

　　Close that lid. I can't abide the tune.

Alan (*producing a key from the box*) And here's the key. (*He closes the lid*)
　　You knew it was there, didn't you?

Emily No.

Alan unlocks the cupboard

Alan Let's see what we've got in here ...

Emily That's private property.

Alan takes a presentation clock out of the cupboard

Alan Dad's long service clock. (*He places it on the cupboard*) I don't know
　　why you don't leave it out.

Emily It doesn't work.

Alan You don't wind it ... (*He looks further into the cupboard*) And what's
　　this? The blue purse. (*He takes a blue purse out of the cupboard and opens
　　it*) With the tissue paper, the little scissors, the cotton wool—and your opal
　　ring.

Emily It never is.

Alan And your crucifix.

Emily How did they get there?

Alan You know how they got there. You put them there. (*Pause*) And there's
　　something else—something I haven't seen before. (*Producing a sapphire
　　ring from the purse*) A sapphire ring. That isn't yours, is it? How did you
　　come by that?

Emily (*glancing desperately at the door*) Put it away!

The door opens and Mrs Lang enters with a tray of tea

Emily closes her eyes and feigns sleep. There is a guilty silence

*Mrs Lang looks from Alan to Emily; then her gaze shifts to the open door of
the cupboard. She puts the tray down*

Mrs Lang So you found the key.

Alan That's not all we found. I think we owe you an apology... (*He turns
　　to Emily and is surprised to find her eyes firmly closed*) We found Mother's
　　jewellery—and this. (*He hands the ring to Mrs Lang*) I'm not sure where
　　it came from...

Mrs Lang It's Bella's.

Alan You don't mean she ...? Mother!

Mrs Lang No, don't disturb her.

Alan She's not asleep.

Mrs Lang (*softly*) I know but she's embarrassed — and confused. They pick things up — they don't realize. We'll say no more about it. What was lost is now found. I know the family will be pleased. I'll put it in the safe ... (*She moves to the door*)

Alan (*following*) I hope you don't think it was intentional. She's never done anything like that before.

Mrs Lang Of course not. It happens all the time. They're like little magpies — always attracted to something that's bright and shiny. But there's no harm in them.

Alan But is this a sign of ... ?

Mrs Lang What?

Alan Failing?

Mrs Lang (*glancing at Emily*) Should we talk about this downstairs?

They exit

Emily slowly opens her eyes. She regards the open cupboard for a moment. She rises stiffly but with no great difficulty and returns the purse to the cupboard and locks it. She puts the cupboard key back in the music box. She returns to her chair and is about to sit when she looks across at May's bed. She crosses and opens the drawer of the bedside table and looks in, closes it then looks for a long moment down at the bed

May enters to retrieve her purse and prayer book. She sees Emily and freezes in surprise. She backs quietly out of the room

Emily hears the sound of the door. She turns sharply. Then she sees the prayer book and picks it up. She looks thoughtfully at the door

CURTAIN

SCENE 2

The bedsitting-room. A few days before Christmas. Early evening

A little tinsel and holly have been draped around the room

Emily is sitting in the wheelchair beside the table, her back to the bathroom. She is wearing a shawl

May emerges from the bathroom in a Victorian-style long skirt and cambric blouse. She moves in and out of the bathroom as she talks

Emily Well, I didn't know anything about it.

May They were all talking about it in the lounge.

Emily Not to me they weren't. Olde Tyme Music Hall?

May By the Operatic. At the Palace. Followed by a fish and chip supper.

Emily I wouldn't have minded the fish and chip supper. (*Sourly*) Operatic. I suppose they'd have expected us to join in the singing.

May I like joining in.

Emily I don't. They're supposed to be entertaining us — not us entertaining them. Why don't they just get on with it? I'm glad I wasn't asked. I'd have been stuck in the middle of a row busting myself. That's what happened last time.

May regards Emily's back for a moment

May Mrs Lang said it was only for the mobile ...

Emily I'll give her mobile. That was a dig at me.

May (*slyly*) And it's five pounds a ticket.

Emily (*aghast*) It never is!

May That's not expensive these days.

Emily Not expensive! They're amateurs. They should do it for nothing.

May It's for a good cause.

Emily We're a good cause. There should have been a reduction.

May That is with a reduction.

Emily It never is.

May The full price is six pounds.

Emily Six pounds! For that lot? I can't believe it. They knocked the scenery over last year. It was a shambles. This woman came on banging a tambourine — supposed to be a gypsy. I've never seen anyone look less like a gypsy. I recognized her from the Rates Office. She banged this tambourine, jumped in the air and came down in the splits.

May That takes some doing.

Emily She didn't manage it. She got stuck.

May She didn't!

Emily Locked. She'd have been there now if they hadn't carried her off.

May Was it serious?

Emily No, she came back later and sang *Scarlet Ribbons* — mind you, she kept forgetting the words. It was dire. And the meal was no better. The café had been vandalized. Mrs Keys got stuck in the lavatory.

May Another one. Don't tell me she was doing the splits?

Emily No — she was stuck to the seat with Superglue.

May She never was.

Emily Those toilets should have been inspected.

May Ours were always immaculate.

Emily She wasn't missed until it was time to pay the bill. Glued to the seat. Never did get her meal. And they didn't make a reduction.

May Poor Mrs Keys. How did they get her off?

Emily Soaked her in hot water — all they could do. It was either that or unscrewing the seat. Left a nasty mark. You can't go anywhere these days.

May There's no respect any more.

Emily Superglue. It should be banned but the government won't act. I could run this country better blindfolded.

May Sounds as if it's a good thing you're not going.

Emily I could have done with the fish and chip supper. I suppose we'll get sandwiches — any excuse not to cook.

May Well, I won't be having sandwiches ...

May passes in front of Emily

What do you think?

Emily (*staring*) Why are you dressed like that?

May Olde Tyme Music Hall.

Emily You didn't tell me you were going.

May Well, I'm telling you now.

Emily You're going without me?

May I was asked, Emily.

Emily They asked you and not me. Where was I?

May Having your perm. You couldn't go anyway. (*Pointedly*) You're immobile ...

Emily So that's it. I'm to be stuck here on my own.

May Emily, you wouldn't have gone.

Emily I wasn't asked.

May You've told me yourself — you can't stand that sort of excitement.

Emily That doesn't mean I won't be bored. (*Muttering*) That's my trouble — I'm bored to death but I can't stand excitement.

May There you are then. (*She takes a brooch from her drawer and pins it to her blouse*)

Emily So I'll be stuck here while you're out gallivanting.

May I won't be gallivanting.

Emily With Vernon Watts.

May No.

Emily Will he be sitting next to you?

May He might.

Emily Watch out for those wandering hands ...

May He doesn't have wandering hands.

Emily I saw him brushing his cigarette ash off your skirt at teatime.

May So what?

Emily It's amazing where that cigarette ash gets. It's been remarked on.

May (*defiantly*) Has it?

Emily I'm surprised Mrs Lang hasn't warned you about him. She warned Bella.

May I'm sure if there's any reason to warn me she'd have done so. Mrs Lang's been like a sister to me since I came here.

Emily (*indignantly*) A sister! And what have I been — your mother?

May No, you've been a blessed nuisance.

Emily Well, you won't have to put up with me much longer. There'll be a single room coming up soon. This winter should see a few of them off.

May Sooner than you think. Mrs James is on the morphine drip.

Emily You've been counting the hours then.

May takes a large Edwardian hat from the wardrobe and fixes it with a large hatpin. She turns

May What do you think?

Emily You look like a lampshade.

May I do not.

Emily If the wind gets up it'll take off.

May It's secured with a large hatpin.

Emily Then you'll take off.

May Mrs Lang thinks it's very becoming.

Emily She would. (*Pause*) So she's been like a sister to you?

May Yes.

Emily You're sure you don't mean a daughter? After all, you're old enough to be her mother. And daughters inherit ...

May What are you getting at?

Emily You're looking at your will again, aren't you?

May That's my business.

Emily There's been a fall out, hasn't there?

May A fall out?

Emily Between you and Frank.

May I've been deeply hurt — you know that. He's been down here to see his friends, he's passed by the bottom of the road — and he's never bothered to call. (*She dabs her eyes*)

Emily If he didn't call how did you know he'd been?

May remains silent

She told you, didn't she?

May Mrs Lang saw Frank in a restaurant; she assumed he'd called.

Emily She shouldn't have told you.

May I'm glad I found out. I know where I stand now. It also explains why they haven't invited me for Christmas. They don't want me. (*She falters*) I sometimes think they went to Scotland just to get away from me. He can't stand the sight of me, Emily.

Emily (*not unkindly*) I wouldn't worry too much about that. It's normal. My lot haven't been able to stand the sight of me for years. In fact two of them emigrated. One to Canada — the far side — and the other to New Zealand — and you can't get much further than that. Not much chance of calling in for afternoon tea.

May But your Alan still comes to see you.

Emily Only when it suits. Still, blood's thicker than water — just remember that when you're looking at your will.

May Mrs Lang wouldn't expect anything.

Emily Don't you believe it. She's been mentioned in more wills than Mother Teresa.

May That's not the impression I've gained. Diana says I should enjoy my money — not leave it to others.

Emily (*staring*) Who's Diana?

May Mrs Lang. She's invited me to call her Diana — in private.

Emily Chase me!

May Diana says I should enjoy myself while I still have my health and strength.

Emily But you haven't got your health and strength, have you?

May (*pointedly*) I don't complain. Not like some people — always going on about their symptoms.

Emily (*indignantly*) These aren't symptoms — these are full-blown ailments. Not that you care — off gallivanting.

May Well, you'd better get used to it. You'll have to do without me when I'm moved downstairs.

Emily I wonder who they'll put in with me?

May Whoever she is — she'll have to be strong.

Emily I knew Mrs Lang would split us up. Don't think I haven't noticed the way she's been taking you out and about. Stately homes and cream teas.

May That's because of my upset. She feels responsible. She's trying to take me out of myself.

Emily And now it's the Olde Tyme Music Hall while I sit here like pork.

May As a matter of fact Diana isn't going. She's staying here to give the staff a break. That's the sort of person she is.

Emily Just Lang to look after the rest of us? The whole organization's breaking down.

May Sally's coming in early.

Emily That wapstraw. Just the two of them — it's a disgrace.

May (*mockingly*) What's the matter — you're not frightened of the prowler, are you?

Emily (*darkly*) No, but you should be.

May What do you mean?

Emily Because the prowler won't be here. He'll be on the coach.

May You mean Vernon, don't you?

Emily I saw him out there, on the fire escape — more than once. He had the key — that's how he got in to see Bella.

May (*shocked*) He didn't.

Emily Didn't he? I heard them. They thought I couldn't but there's nothing wrong with my hearing.

May Why didn't he use the door like everyone else?

Emily At dead of night? Lang didn't approve. (*Pause*) And he's still got the key, May...

May I don't think you should blacken a person's character like this, Emily.

Emily He was taking her money.

May What!

Emily And she found out.

May I don't believe it.

Emily He ran her errands — nothing was too much trouble. He was supposed to collect her pension and pay it in but he never did. He was drawing out.

May Then she would have known. There are such things as bank statements, Emily.

Emily laughs

What?

Emily (*nodding*) Look in the back of the clock.

May stares at Emily and moves to the clock on the cupboard. She opens the back of the clock and takes a piece of paper from it

May It's Bella's bank statement.

Emily It's more than that. It's evidence. You're a businesswoman, May — what do you make of it?

May There's hardly any money left.

Emily I know.

May And some large withdrawals.

Emily Vernon Watts. I remember that statement coming because she hardly ever had any post. He saw to that. She went pale — and then angry — and then said, "Wait until I see Vernon". She died that night. When I woke up the room was icy cold but not as cold as Bella, poor soul. I heard Lang talking to the doctor. There were contusions ... Know what they are? Bruises.

May You're talking wildly, Emily. And why now? Why haven't you produced this statement before?

Emily Because I'd forgotten where I'd put it. Besides, it's evidence — I'm not letting it go.

May If you believe all this why haven't you told Mrs Lang or Alan?

Emily Because they wouldn't have believed me, not without that paper — and I'd forgotten where I'd put it. My memory's not what it was. And there's another reason. (*Pause*) They think I'm cuckoo.

May Of course they don't.

Emily Oh, yes they do. I've seen the way they look. I've heard the way they talk. (*She holds May's arm in a strong grip*) But you don't, do you?

May No.

Emily You're the first person here I've met who I can trust. And you're a businesswoman. They'll listen to you.

May I'm not saying anything. Don't involve me. This should be handed in.

Emily Put it back.

May hesitates for a moment and then returns the statement to the back of the clock

There's a knock on the door and Sally enters

There is a guilty silence

Sally (*coldly*) I've come to take you down. Your Alan's here. He's on his way to get a pizza so he's in a hurry.

Emily A pizza? Doesn't she ever cook?

May I think a pizza makes a nice change.

Emily They would if you could chew them.

Sally (*regarding Emily's hair*) Do you want me to put a comb through that perm?

Emily Certainly not. I didn't have a perm so you could straighten it. It's got to last. The money she charges. It's daylight robbery. I told her. Who's paying for the electricity?

Sally Well, you're not.

Emily I am — indirectly.

Sally makes to push Emily out of the room in her wheelchair, but notices the clock and stops

Sally Your clock's stopped. Do you want me to wind it?

Emily No. (*Quickly*) I'll need my clean cardigan — it's perishing down there.

Sally I'll get it.

Sally crosses to the music box and takes out the key. Emily watches her with eyebrows raised. Sally unlocks the cupboard and takes out the cardigan

Emily (*muttering*) I'll have to find a new place for that...
May (*hastily*) How's the new house coming along, Sally?
Sally You wouldn't believe it.

Sally pushes Emily back towards her bed and settles down to talk. Emily looks indignant. During the following she pushes the button to ring the bell

We were there yesterday. I was pointing out the PVC windows and discussing swish curtains and he suddenly said: "Do you realize that one day this won't be here — the house or the garden?"
May He never did.
Sally He did. "Not just the house — the whole estate will probably be a nuclear swamp."
May The things he comes out with.
Sally I told him, that may be true but that's no reason why we should go rented. Then do you know what he said? "We're just specks on the cosmos."
May (*incredulously*) Specks on the cosmos? I've never heard anyone called that before.
Sally "What's it all for?" he said. "In the inter-galactic time scale ten seconds is almost the same as forty years."
Emily (*grimly*) It is when you're waiting to go downstairs.

Sally darts a sharp glance at Emily

May Sounds as if he'd get cold feet again, Sally.
Sally Then he said, "What's marriage anyway? A few words mumbled over you by a priest; taking vows no-one intends to keep." I said he'd better keep them — I'm paying for this lot.
May Good for you, Sally.

There is a sharp tap on the door. Mrs Lang enters

Mrs Lang Sally, I asked you to hurry. Mr Baines is waiting.
Sally I am hurrying.
Mrs Lang Then why was Emily forced to to ring her bell?
Sally (*surprised*) What!
Mrs Lang Not a thing she'd do lightly.

Emily looks innocent

What happens when you come up here, Sally? You enter a room and suddenly it's Wednesday.

Sally It's Tuesday, Mrs Lang.

Mrs Lang I know it's Tuesday but it'll be Wednesday before you get Mrs Baines down there.

Emily I'd be down there quicker if there was less talking ...

Sally scowls

Mrs Lang Your hair looks nice, Emily. I wish mine would take like that.

Emily sniffs disdainfully and pats her hair

Sally, I'd like a word with you later.

Sally wheels Emily out

(*Turning and smiling at May*) You look a picture, May.

May Is the hat all right? It doesn't look silly?

Mrs Lang Of course not.

May Emily says I look like a lampshade.

Mrs Lang Take no notice. I warned you about Emily before you came in here. (*She regards May for a moment*) Are things getting a little fraught?

May Diana, sometimes she frightens me.

Mrs Lang She frightens everyone. (*Pause*) It'll be cold out tonight. Should we have a little nip?

May (*hesitating*) Oh, you know about that.

Mrs Lang May, we don't have a rule against it.

Mrs Lang fetches two glasses from the bathroom as May takes out the sherry. May pours them each a glass of sherry during the following

May It's for my heart.

Mrs Lang Is it?

May is silent for a moment

May No. It got worse after Harry died. I needed something to get me through. I needed it to do the big things — now I need it to do the small things.

Mrs Lang At least you do them. The only thing I worry about is you doing it in secret.

May makes to put the bottle away

Leave the bottle out, May.

May Do you think I should?

Mrs Lang Yes.

May leaves the bottle out

May What will Emily say?

Mrs Lang Never mind Emily. A drop of sherry won't kill you, May.

May No, there isn't time for that.

Mrs Lang What do you mean?

May I'll be gone long before that.

Mrs Lang You're being morbid, May.

May Everything is going by at such a rush.

Mrs Lang Here? Most of our residents say time drags.

May It does but it drags so quickly. I know why Emily doesn't wind up that clock. That's what I'd like to do — stop time, just for an hour — just to get my breath.

Mrs Lang May, I didn't know you felt like that.

May I broke a mirror in my handbag the other day. I thought "seven years' bad luck" — then I thought how could seven years be bad luck at my age?

Mrs Lang smiles

I feel lucky if I get through the night.

Mrs Lang What is it, May? Is it Emily?

May She gets me so agitated.

Mrs Lang You mustn't let her. The trouble is as we get older we worry more and more about less and less. Just remember she's a sick old lady.

May (*quietly*) Not so sick …

Mrs Lang Why do you say that?

May remains silent

May, you remember our little agreement — before you came in here? That you'd let me know if there was a change in Emily's behaviour — any further deterioration.

May If she found out we were talking like this she'd never forgive me. She trusts me. She'd be so angry.

Mrs Lang May, she can't hurt you.

May Can't she? She hasn't deteriorated. She isn't bedridden. Diana, she can walk.

Mrs Lang What? But Emily hasn't walked in years — not without assistance.

May I found her standing by my bed. She can walk.

Mrs Lang Then why should she pretend she couldn't?

May I don't know. Do you believe me?

Mrs Lang I don't know what to believe. (*She hesitates*) It would explain one thing. How she came by Bella's ring.

May (*shocked*) She took Bella's ring?

Mrs Lang She could have taken it after Bella died.

May She took a ring from a dead body? Oh, my God!

Mrs Lang All I know is that Bella always wore the ring.

May (*after a pause*) Diana, were there bruises on Bella's face when they found her?

Mrs Lang Bella died from emphysema.

May Emily thinks otherwise.

Mrs Lang I know. She blames Vernon Watts. She's always looking for someone to blame. And that's because she blames herself. I thought it was significant that she wouldn't go to Bella's funeral. I thought it was the sign of a bad conscience, May.

May (*after a pause*) She says she has evidence.

Mrs Lang What evidence?

May There's another reason why Emily doesn't wind the clock. Look in the back.

Mrs Lang stares at her and then crosses and takes the statement from the back of the clock. She studies it

Mrs Lang It's Bella's bank statement. We've been looking for this.

May Emily said she became distressed when she opened it — that she was going to see Vernon about it.

Mrs Lang There's only a few pounds in here.

May That's what distressed her. Emily said that Vernon went to the bank for her. That he took her money.

Mrs Lang Vernon didn't go to the bank. He couldn't. He couldn't get beyond the gates. He has chronic asthma. Sally did all his errands. And although he's a smart little man you may observe that his cuffs are frayed and his trousers are shiny. He certainly hasn't had Bella's money. And there's something else — he wasn't here when Bella died.

May What?

Mrs Lang He was staying with family. And the reason why the balance is so low is quite understandable. Bella was very generous both to her family and friends; she was also very confused. She'd forget, find the money had gone and then become indignant. It had happened before.

May That's a relief. I just wish Emily would leave it alone.

Mrs Lang I'll put this with the rest of Bella's papers …

Alan pushes Emily into the room in her wheelchair

Mrs Lang slips the statement into her pocket

Alan You'll miss your sandwiches.
Emily I'm not staying down there — it's perishing ... (*She breaks off and regards May and Mrs Lang suspiciously. She notes the bottle and the glasses and sniffs*)

Mrs Lang picks up the glasses and moves to Alan

Mrs Lang Mr Baines, did you notice if the coach had arrived?
Alan It's outside the front door.
Mrs Lang We'd better get down there, May.

May exits hurriedly

(*Turning to Alan*) I'm sorry your mother won't be going. But never mind, tomorrow we're having a turkey and tinsel evening followed by super bingo. And in the afternoon Mrs Skinner's going to reveal her secrets with marzipan. Won't that be fun?

She is rewarded by another disdainful sniff from Emily

Mrs Lang exits

Emily Close that door.

Alan closes the door

Alan What's the matter?
Emily Don't you think those two looked shifty?
Alan Everyone looks shifty to you.
Emily I suppose it's because they'd been drinking. May's always liked a drop but it shouldn't be encouraged. I don't want her singing in the middle of the night.
Alan I thought you liked May.
Emily She's all right.
Alan Be careful, you might say something nice about her in a minute. (*Pause*) Well, the door's closed — what did you want to tell me?
Emily I want to get out of here — before the trouble starts.
Alan (*alarmed*) You're not getting out of here! What trouble?
Emily The trouble that's coming when Vernon Watts finds out I'm on to him.

Alan Not Vernon Watts again!

Emily I don't want him coming up here and cutting my throat because you and Lang won't take action.

Alan What action? What are you talking about? You're not being rational. You can't leave here because there's nowhere for you to go. You can't come to us.

Emily Why not? Don't tell me you're decorating again.

Alan Mother, it's Christmas. We've got a houseful. And Judith's not well.

Emily She's never well when I'm mentioned. I haven't been in that house since your father died.

Alan Judith's not well, Mother — that's why I'm fetching pizza.

Emily So I can go to the wall, can I?

Alan (*sighing*) I don't know where this wall is you keep going to but if it's here it seems pretty damned comfortable to me.

Emily You don't have to live here. Well, if I can't come to you I shall have to book into a hotel.

Alan Don't be ridiculous.

Emily Then I'll just have to come to you.

Alan I've just told you. Don't you ever listen? There's no room. The kids are at home. Where would you sleep?

Emily Put a bed in the kitchen. She never uses it.

Alan Don't call Judith she! Her name's Judith for God's sake! Where do you expect us to put you — in the garage?

Emily Well, I would be at home there, wouldn't I? Along with my dressing-table, my marble washstand and my green and gold wicker linen basket. If they're still there. If they haven't been sold or given away.

Alan Of course they're still there! (*Pause*) Look, Mother — you know what this is all about. You're unhappy here and I'm sorry. But I can't do anything about it — not at the moment. So there's no point in stirring up trouble. All this about Vernon Watts is pure fantasy.

Emily Suppose I said I'd got evidence and that May Brewer agrees with me?

Alan May?

Emily That makes a difference, doesn't it? She's not cuckoo — she's a businesswoman — and she thinks there's cause for concern.

Alan (*after a pause*) What evidence?

Emily I'm going to give you a chance to make a name for yourself. Look in the back of your dad's clock.

Alan stares, then moves to the clock and opens the back

You'll find a bank statement.

Alan There's nothing here.

Emily What!

Alan There's nothing here.

Emily (*faltering*) But it was there — I know it was.

Alan It's not there, Mother, because you imagined it. It's not your fault. You're confused. You do a lot of sleeping these days. You dream. Sometimes the dream seems real. Then you wake up and you think what you've dreamt has actually happened … (*He pulls Emily's shawl closer about her*)

Emily closes her eyes wearily

Look at you — you're exhausted.

Emily (*wearily; burying her face inside the shawl*) I know it was there — I know it was …

Alan You're tired. Try and get some rest. (*Pause*) Do you want me to wind the clock?

Silence

That clock hasn't gone since Dad died. You all stopped at the same time, didn't you? Dad, you, the clock. I could start the clock again but not you. Because you won't try.

We hear the sound of the departing coach

You won't lighten up. They haven't left you behind because you're immobile. I saw the wheelchairs going on to the coach. It's because of the way you are. The way you've always been. I still remember you polishing the furniture. Polishing — polishing — polishing. And never smiling. Even now when I smell furniture polish I feel depressed. The trouble is you never believed anyone loved you — and in the end — they didn't. (*Pause*) Mother?

Emily's head drops forward. Alan tiptoes to the door

Sally enters

Alan puts a finger to his lips and exits

Sally closes the door and regards Emily coldly

Sally You've got me into trouble again, haven't you? Pressing that bell — you never press that bell. Always complaining. I'd like to give you something to complain about.

Sally pushes Emily back in her chair. Emily's eyes remain closed. Sally takes one of her cushions and begins to plump it

During the following, May enters and stands in the doorway, watching Sally

This is the only time you're no trouble. When you're asleep. You could do with a long sleep, like Bella. She's no trouble — not any more. Although she was an angel compared with you. (*Smiling*) Well, she's an angel now. (*She plumps the pillow savagely*) If I lose my job because of you ... With all my expenses. You've had your time — let me have mine. You know what you are? A waste of space. You should have gone years ago. I can never understand why the penalty's the same for snuffing out the old. The young, yes — they've got their whole lives before them. But someone with only two or three years — that shouldn't be a serious offence ... (*She places the cushion almost playfully in front of Emily's face*) After all, what are you taking away? A few months of aches and pains and moans and groans. I'd be doing you a favour. I don't think it's even worth probation. Or perhaps the murderer should serve the same time the murdered person was expected to live — which in your case is not long. No, I still think probation. It wouldn't take much, would it? You're half-way there already... (*She glares down at Emily for a while longer and then realizes that May is watching her from the open door*)

May and Sally regard each other for a moment. Sally slips the cushion deftly behind Emily's head

May, I thought you were going on the trip.
May I felt faint. It must have been the night air ...

May continues staring at Sally. Sally makes a display of making Emily comfortable

Sally I'll see Mrs Lang. She'll probably give you something.

Sally exits

May Well, who'd have believed it? (*She glances at Emily*) I'm surprised you slept through that.
Emily (*without opening her eyes*) Who's asleep?

CURTAIN

ACT II

The same. Two hours later

The two bedside lamps are on as well as the overhead lights

Emily and May are in their dressing-gowns. May has a glass of sherry and is putting away the clothes she was wearing earlier, watched by Emily. May pauses over her hat

May Where's my hatpin?

Emily What?

May My hatpin's gone.

Emily Has it? I'm not surprised. Things are always disappearing here.

May Who'd want a three inch Edwardian hatpin?

Emily You probably lost it out there. You looked a wreck when you came back.

May I wasn't well. It was the night air.

Emily It was the sherry.

May It wasn't! (*Pause*) Actually, it was neither.

Emily Then what was it?

May It was when I was going on the coach. Vernon was sitting next to an empty seat. He grinned and patted it with his hand. And I swear I heard someone say, "Look at the love birds". And suddenly I couldn't be doing with it. That's why I got off. (*She sips her sherry mournfully*)

Emily Well, take my advice — don't have any more of that. You'll start singing.

May I will not.

Emily You always do. *We'll Meet Again* — complete with sobs. I wouldn't have minded but the next day it's: "Why did I do it? What must they have thought? I wish I could put it out of my mind."

May (*quietly*) I wish I could forget a lot of things, Emily.

Emily I know. It's always the same with you and me. The next day you're trying to forget what you said — and I'm trying to remember.

May Then your mind is playing tricks?

Emily (*sharply*) I never said that.

May But your memory's not what it is.

Emily I remember you putting that statement in the clock and now it's not there …

May (*turning away*) I don't know why you object to my singing. They say I have a lovely voice.

Emily Who says?

May Everyone.

Emily I've never heard them. Anyway, it's not much of a compliment around here — they're all deaf.

May I mean Mrs Lang and the staff.

Emily I don't hold with all this singing. That's why I stopped going to church. They've taken over. It's full of warblers these days. I don't think God wants to hear all that warbling.

May (*indignantly*) I don't warble. The staff say it's nice to listen to old songs and hear about the war.

Emily broods on this for a moment

Emily I enjoyed the war.

May (*drily*) I thought you would.

Emily Bill had plenty of overtime. We were out most nights. Mainly the *Cross Keys* but sometimes the *Sun Inn*. (*She becomes nostalgic*) I had a little sailor hat, a swagger jacket and a pleated skirt. I looked as smart as paint. Only one thing marred my appearance — my teeth. I dropped them in the sink at the outbreak and chipped them. Well, they cost a fortune to replace in those days — even if you could find someone to do them. Bill said "Why bother? We could be blown up tomorrow." I told him, "It looks as if I've been blown up today." But he was always a bit on the mean side. So I went through the war with this sort of crooked smile. Bill said it made me look interesting. All I know is it made me look chipped.

May Well, the war was a great source of unhappiness to me. When I think of it I always feel sad. Those sobs aren't put on, Emily. They rise in my throat — I can't help it. (*Pause*) I had a bad experience.

Emily I know.

May (*staring*) You do?

Emily Walter somebody, wasn't it?

May Harrison. How did you know about that? No-one knew about that.

Emily I did. And I wasn't the only one.

May Oh my God.

Emily He was billeted here, wasn't he? Just before they went over.

May Yes. Harry was on nights. It was very brief. They were under orders.

Emily Yes. I remember the night before they went over. They had leave. The town was full of red berets and the sound of boots. And not a window broken.

May Discipline was strict — not like today.

Emily Good thing it was. I don't know if they frightened the Germans — they certainly did me. I was glad they were on our side. The sky was red too — as red as their berets — blood red. And they all looked so serious.

May They had a right to be. At least Walter had. I've never seen his grave. They put a memorial in the park. I know it backwards. "In memory of those who went forth, endured hardship and finally passed out of the sight of men by the path of sacrifice and the gate of death."

Emily Now it's covered in graffiti.

May Well, he certainly passed out of my sight.

Emily Don't start blubbing.

May If I tell you something, will you keep it to yourself? It's something I've never told anyone. Our Frank isn't Harry's — he's Walter's.

Emily I know.

May You don't!

Emily I do. He never looked like Harry — never had his features.

May (*sighing*) I know. It always worried me. I dressed them the same: the same knitted sweaters, parted Frank's hair just like Harry's — but it never worked. People were always asking: "Who does he take after?"

Emily Does your Frank know?

May No.

Emily Are you going to tell him?

May At this stage?

Emily Be something to talk about. That's the trouble when they visit — the lack of conversation.

May It's not a talking point, Emily! Although you're right. When Frank used to visit he was always looking at his watch.

Emily Well, it would certainly stop him looking at his watch.

May He doesn't come any more so what's the point. He doesn't care.

Emily We've lived too long, May. They've begun to see all our faults. We should have had the good sense to die before they noticed them. Our Alan's now blaming me for the smell of furniture polish. The week before it was why did I give him aspirin covered in jam? He says he can't eat jam now without tasting aspirins! You end up getting the blame for everything. Still, I suppose they'll all be at the funeral — weeping and wailing — and then back for a nice ham tea.

May studies Emily for a moment

May Emily, why didn't you go to Bella's funeral?

Emily I don't like funerals.

May Vernon went.

Emily That was remorse.

May Vernon didn't have Bella's money. Mrs Lang was right. His cuffs are frayed. I noticed tonight. And he didn't go to the bank for Bella. It was Sally.

Emily Sally?

May And Vernon wasn't even here that night. He was staying with family.

Emily What?

May So you see you were wrong.

Emily Am I? It's obvious. They're in it together.

May What?

Emily Didn't you say Sally was looking daggers at me tonight?

May Well, yes. When I came in she had this cushion in her hands and she was ...

Emily About to finish me off.

May No. I don't know.

Emily They're in it together. Vernon Watts is the mastermind — she does the dirty work. He was supposed to get you out of the way tonight while she had a go at me.

May That's insane.

Emily Is it? If you hadn't come back I'd have been done for. You said if looks could kill.

May Looks — that's all.

Emily She knew where the key was. You saw that. That was how she was able to put Bella's ring in my things.

May Why should she do that?

Emily To incriminate me — to make me look crazy as a coot. She probably took the bank statement as well.

May She didn't.

Emily How do you know?

May (*after a hesitation*) She wouldn't.

Emily Wouldn't she. You hear the way she was talking to me — like someone demented. And we always wondered where she got her money from. Now we know. She was on that night. She was the last person to see Bella alive. And don't forget, she tried to drown me.

May (*sighing*) There are moments, Emily, when I wish she'd succeeded.

Emily And she does that kicking thing.

May What kicking thing?

Emily It's Japanese. It's like wrestling only they kick each other. Is it karaoke?

May Karate.

Emily Whatever. She and Ian go to the Leisure Centre every Tuesday and kick seven bells out of each other. Supposed to relax them. I wouldn't like her kicking me — not with those feet.

May She wouldn't.

Emily Wouldn't she? What's going to happen tonight when Lang's gone and the others aren't back? She could kick us to her heart's content.

May She's got nothing against me. It's you she doesn't like.

Emily Well, I wouldn't take too much comfort in that. You're a witness. She could finish you off while she's in the mood.

May Don't get me worked up, Emily — I can't stand it.
Emily You'd better go down there right now and tell Lang of our suspicions.
May *Your* suspicions. Why should I? Why don't you tell your Alan?
Emily Because he won't listen. He hasn't listened to me in years. But they'll
   listen to you, May. They respect you.
May Well, they won't respect me for long. They'll think I'm mad.
Emily Let me ask you this. You said you saw the way she looked at me. (*She
   grasps May's hand*) Do you feel safe in here tonight?

May looks uncertainly at Emily

May No.
Emily Then have a word with Lang.
May I'll speak to Mrs Lang but I won't promise anything. (*Almost backing
   towards the door*) Because when I get out of this room — things always
   look different.

May exits

*Emily waits for a moment and then stands and crosses to the music box. She
takes May's hatpin from the music box and pushes it inside the lapel of her
dressing-gown. She returns to her chair and sits, arms folded, regarding the
door*

*There are sounds of an approach, off. Emily hears the sounds and stiffens.
There is a knock on the door. Emily stares*

Alan enters

Emily What are you doing here?
Alan I'm on my way home with a fourteen inch pizza and a cannelloni —
   and they're both cooling rapidly — so I haven't much time. I just want to
   be sure you won't cause any trouble.
Emily I'm not causing any trouble.
Alan There'll be trouble if Vernon Watts finds out what you're saying about
   him. The only reason he wouldn't take you to court is because you're not
   fit to plead. Do you want to end up in a secure wing, Mother? Because that's
   where you'll be if you don't stop this.
Emily I don't know what you're talking about.
Alan (*lowering his voice*) Aren't you telling people that Vernon Watts killed
   Bella Bottomley?
Emily No.
Alan You're not?
Emily No.

Alan I must say that's a relief.

Emily It was Sally.

Alan What!

Emily Of course he was the instigator — but she did it.

Alan Now there's two of them!

Emily Yes.

Alan They've formed a gang.

Emily If you can call it a gang.

Alan (*shaking his head*) Mother, they'll have to change your tablets.

Emily What do you mean?

Alan You're suffering from delusions.

Emily Am I? Well, I'm not the only person to think it. Ask May Brewer. You'd believe her, wouldn't you? She's down there right now. She's having a word with Lang. Mind you, they'll probably close ranks — they usually do: vested interests. Still, she might listen to May.

Alan Do you really believe that? She's not having a word with Mrs Lang. Can't you see she's humouring you?

Emily (*staring*) Humouring me?

Alan Yes. If she is having a word with Mrs Lang — it's to ask for a move.

Emily She does want a move.

Alan There you are then.

Emily Humouring me. That's what Bella used to do — humour me.

Alan That's what everyone does. They humour you.

Emily So she's in with them, is she?

Alan She's not in with them! There's no them. There's just you!

Emily I knew you'd take their side against mine. I've lived too long that's my trouble. You've never taken my side.

Alan And when did you ever take my side? I was always in the wrong. It was always, "Wipe that smile off your face — you never know what's round the corner."

Emily You don't.

Alan Do you remember when I was young — I'd get up in the morning laughing. And do you know what you'd say? "Laugh before breakfast — cry before supper." So I stopped laughing. Then you wanted to know why I was so bloody miserable in the morning. My family want to know why I'm so miserable in the morning.

Emily You are miserable in the morning.

Alan And whose fault is that? You weren't just miserable in the morning. You filled the house with gloom; washing, ironing, polishing — everything was a penance.

Emily My goodness! We'll be getting back to the aspirins in the jam in a minute.

Alan And now you're doing it here.

Emily I didn't want to come here. You wouldn't have put your dad here.
Alan Dad would have been happy here. They'd have loved him. Because he
    liked people — he never made them feel guilty. Well, you're not going to
    make me feel guilty any more. Thank God I'm over that.

Emily eyes Alan shrewdly

Emily If you don't feel guilty — what are you doing here?

Alan stares at Emily for a moment

Alan You're right! I'm feeling guilty. I've got pizza and a cannelloni cooling
    out there and I'm standing here feeling guilty. Well, it's not me who should
    feel guilty. (*Pause*) You want to know who killed Bella? I'll tell you. You
    did. You wore her out — just like you wore Dad out.
Emily I never wore your dad out.
Alan He waited on you hand and foot. It was "Bill do this" and "Bill do that".
    Always telling him to straighten himself up and look lively.

Emily looks stricken for a moment

Emily That wasn't wearing him out — that was keeping him young.
Alan And you were keeping Bella young? And are you keeping May young?
Emily I didn't wear him out. I just didn't want him to be ill. I didn't want him
    to be ill and die.
Alan But he did die. And so did Bella. And now it's May.
Emily Humouring me?
Alan Yes. (*He crosses to the door and turns*) Oh, and there was something
    else you did. I've just remembered. When I was small and I was constipated.
    You stuffed pieces of soap up my backside. Have you any idea how that
    felt?

Alan exits, slamming the door

The sound of Alan talking to Sally comes from off stage

Emily sits upright straining to listen, watching the door

Sally enters with a bottle of eyedrops. She eyes Emily malevolently

Emily's hand strays to the hatpin in her lapel

Sally He says you're disturbed.

Emily Who does?
Sally Your Alan. What have you been saying to him?
Emily Never you mind.
Sally Have you been complaining about me?
Emily No.
Sally I've had two warnings already.
Emily I'm surprised you haven't had more.
Sally Another one and I'm out. That would suit you, wouldn't it?
Emily What have you come for?
Sally To do your eyedrops.
Emily Well, don't poke my eye out.
Sally I've never touched your eye.
Emily Then why is it bloodshot?
Sally Perhaps it's been at too many keyholes.

*Sally tilts Emily's head back and administers the eyedrops during the
following*

May enters

Sally's mood lightens

   Feeling better, May?
May A little …
Emily Never mind about her — let's have a little concentration. Ouch!
Sally Did Mrs Lang give you something?
May No.
Sally Only I noticed you were talking to her. Nothing wrong is there?
May No, she was just concerned. (*Hurriedly*) How's the decorating coming
   along? Will you be finished?
Sally We've run out of money.
Emily Really. I thought you had plenty.

Sally concludes the eyedrop routine

Sally We've had to defer the fitted bedroom in the oak veneer.
Emily I could put you in the way of a dressing-table with an oval mirror —
   good as new — and a marble washstand.
Sally (*sneering*) A marble washstand. I wouldn't thank you for it. Our
   bathroom's en suite: twin hand basins, shower, bidet — all in magnolia. Ian
   wanted avocado but I said who has avocado these days?
Emily Who has a bidet?
Sally We do.

Emily Do you know how to use it?

Sally Of course.

Emily You must have spent a fortune. I don't know how you do it.

May (*hastily*) I'm sure that's none of our business, Emily.

Sally Well, just between you and me and the gate post — I had a stroke of luck.

Emily You mean someone died...

May frowns at Emily

Sally Yes. My granny.

Emily Amy Billing! I didn't know about that. It wasn't in the paper.

Sally We didn't want to arouse the interest of the authorities — there was some dispute over rent and rates. So we kept it quiet.

Emily Poor old Amy. I was at school with her.

Sally She didn't suffer. She went on Saturday lunchtime with the doctor in attendance.

Emily (*suspiciously*) He didn't inject her, did he?

Sally No, he was taking her pulse. She was surrounded by the family.

May She couldn't have wished for more.

Sally Do you know what her last words were? (*Solemnly*) "What's happened to those sausages?"

May They never were.

Sally Her last words. "What's happened to those sausages?" Lucid to the end.

Emily Sausages?

Sally She loved sausages.

Emily So do I. But you can't get them here. Not in their skins.

Sally "What's happened to those sausages?" Those were her last words — and then she died.

Emily (*grimly*) Hungry.

May At least it didn't affect her appetite.

Sally It didn't affect the family's either. While the doctor was ringing the undertaker they sat down and scoffed the lot.

May They didn't.

Sally They did.

Emily That doesn't surprise me.

Sally Then they started looking for her money.

May They never did.

Sally While she was still in the house, before she was cold. They made a complete search. They even lifted her up to see if she was sitting on it.

May That's disgraceful.

Sally Then there was a row because the unemployed said they should have more than the rest because their needs were greater. Then there was a fight over the new television.

May But they didn't find anything?

Sally (*smiling*) There was nothing to find — because it was in my bank account. Granny had given it to me for safe keeping. She wanted me to have it. I was the only one who visited.

Emily How much?

May Emily!

Sally (*proudly*) Twenty thousand pounds.

Emily What! Amy Billing? I didn't think she had tuppence to bless herself with. She must have owed a lot of rent and rates.

Sally She'd been on disability for years.

Emily Disability. She was scrubbing floors till she was eighty.

May And the family never had any suspicion?

Sally No — although they've been giving me some very funny looks since I've started spending the money — but then so have you ...

Sally exits

Emily and May sit in silence for a moment

May Well. What do you think of that?

Emily I hope I find something more interesting to say than "What's happened to those sausages?"

May What?

Emily For my last words. I think that's trivial.

May Well, she didn't know they were going to be her last words, did she? You don't know when you're going to go. (*Pause*) Still, it explains where she got the money from. It puts a different complexion on things.

Emily No, it doesn't. There's never enough money for people who want bidets, and showers, and twin hand basins. More wants more, May. What did you say to Lang?

May (*after a hesitation*) Well ...

Emily Go on.

May I said we were a little disturbed by Sally's manner.

Emily Is that all?

May And I wondered if her attitude was anything to do with the fact that you suspected her — along with Vernon Watts.

Emily Is that it?

May Yes.

Emily You didn't say any more?

May It sounds ridiculous, Emily. And she looked at me very strangely.

Emily She looked at you strangely! And that stopped you?

May (*after a hesitation*) That wasn't what stopped me. I saw something that made me feel I couldn't say any more. It took my breath away. She was wearing Bella's ring.

Emily What?

May Mrs Lang was wearing Bella's ring.

Emily So that's it! They're all in it together.

May No!

Emily It's a conspiracy. They're sharing the spoils. Picking over the carcasses like a flock of vultures. And who's going to ask any questions? They're waiting for us to die anyway. And if we don't die fast enough — they hasten the process.

May There could be a simple explanation.

Emily What simple explanation?

May It could be a bequest.

Emily Bella wouldn't make a will. She told me. She had a morbid feeling about it.

May Perhaps the family said she could have it.

Emily Bella didn't have a family. She was alone in the world. The perfect victim.

May You're getting carried away again, Emily.

Emily I should have known. Lang's always been a closed door but she has one weakness — jewellery. You should see her when the trustees visit — all dressed up and dripping with the jewellery of the dead. I'd hide those diamonds if I were you. Has she admired them?

May Well, yes.

Emily You'll be next.

May Emily, you've got things wrong. You live in a dream world. Bella did have family. Mrs Lang told me. She was going to give them the bank statement ——

Emily (*sharply*) What was that?

May (*after a hesitation*) She was going to give them the statement.

Emily So it was you. You gave it to her.

May I thought it was for the best.

Emily So you were put here to spy.

May No.

Emily You're in with them, aren't you?

May Oh, yes, I'm in with them. There's Vernon, Sally, Mrs Lang and me. We're all at it. In fact it was me who did Bella in — just so I could share this room with you. My God!

Emily studies May

Emily You were humouring me, weren't you? You were telling Lang everything I said.

May No. Emily, would I have told you about the ring if I were in with them?

Emily I don't know. I don't know anything any more. All I know is you're all against me. That's what Bella did — she humoured me.

May Emily, there could be a simple explanation — that's all I'm saying. We've too much time on our hands — the mind begins to play tricks. That's the trouble with old age.

Emily sits silent for a moment

Emily That's not the trouble with old age. The trouble with old age is the plumbing ... Give me a hand.
May Ring the bell.
Emily I wouldn't give them the satisfaction.
May It's a pity you can't walk, isn't it?

Emily darts May a glance

Emily You told her that too, didn't you?
May I don't know what you're talking about.

May assists Emily out of her chair and into the bathroom

May returns and checks her hat once more. She begins to search Emily's drawers for the hatpin. She opens the music box. It begins to play and she shuts the lid abruptly. She continues her search, all the time glancing nervously at the bathroom

Suddenly there's a tap on the door and Mrs Lang enters. She is wearing a raincoat

May starts violently. Mrs Lang regards her curiously

Mrs Lang I'm going now, May. Are you all right?
May I think so.

Mrs Lang takes a bottle of tablets from her pocket

Mrs Lang You looked strained. (*She glances at the bathroom*) Has she been playing up?
May You could say that.

Mrs Lang gently closes the bathroom door

Mrs Lang I thought this might happen. It's my fault. I haven't been fair to you, May.
May It's such a strain, Diana.

Mrs Lang I know, but I thought if she could have a companion, someone who she could talk to, talk her fantasies out — then she wouldn't harm herself or anyone else. I thought you'd be a breath of fresh air in here — someone sane and rational.

May I don't feel sane and rational at the moment.

Mrs Lang (*smiling*) I realize that. That was a very strange conversation we had a few moments ago.

May I know. It sounded strange to me.

Mrs Lang I know Emily dislikes Sally but that doesn't make her a thief. She's clumsy and she's stupid and I'd love to get rid of her but I've never found her dishonest. I don't know where her money came from but it certainly didn't come from Bella. That's why we have to be discreet. Sally is in a special position — the slightest suspicion could ruin her. And if these wild fancies of Emily were believed it would be considered a breach of trust — Sally would be judged more harshly. Things sometimes get out of hand — people think there's no smoke without fire … There's the reputation of the home to consider — if Sally went to prison.

May Prison!

Mrs Lang It has been known. Would you want that?

May No.

Mrs Lang Bella was very generous. She gave to everyone. Sally may have had something — she may have difficulty proving it was a gift … It could look bad. But we shouldn't condemn her because of that. (*She studies May for a moment and smiles*) Take this ring for example. I've noticed you've looked at it several times. You recognize it, don't you?

May Not really. Well, I thought it looked like Bella's.

Mrs Lang It is Bella's. She begged me to have it when she was alive. I refused. She was very distressed. So I promised to wear it one day. This happens to be the day. I was very fond of Bella. She knew that. She wanted to be remembered, we all want to be remembered, May. "Remember when I am gone away / Gone far away into the silent land … " Wouldn't you want to be remembered when you go into that silent land?

May Yes, I suppose I would.

Mrs Lang Still, I suppose this looks bad too …

May No.

Mrs Lang (*smiling*) Don't worry, I shan't keep it — it's in with her effects. I don't need a ring to remember Bella. It'll go to the family.

May But Emily said there wasn't any family.

Mrs Lang But there is. It's just that Bella disowned them. There was a quarrel that was never mended. They never visited. Rather like you and Frank. Attitudes hardened. I implored her to make it up but she wouldn't. Promise me you won't be like that, May.

May That's in Frank's hands.

Mrs Lang No. The young are thoughtless. Don't be too proud, May. Don't be like Bella. Don't let the sun set on your wrath. Bella waited for hours in reception waiting for them to call. Waiting for a car to take her out and about. She never said a word. But I knew. Well, they'll come now but I'm afraid it's too late. (*She rises, places some tablets by Emily's bed and pours some water from a decanter*)

May Perhaps if Emily was to meet the family? She might understand — it might put her mind at rest.

Mrs Lang It's a thought I suppose ... (*She returns to where May is sitting. She moves closer and lowers her voice*) But there's something you have to realize about Emily. She's going slowly but inevitably insane.

May I know.

Mrs Lang And the insane mind dwells on what fascinates it most. It's called an obsession — a morbid obsession. Emily is obsessed with Bella's death. Why I'm not sure. But it couldn't have been easy for her waking up that morning and finding Bella dead. For some reason she wants to blame someone. Now it's Sally.

May She says Sally was working late that night. That she was the last person to see Bella alive.

Mrs Lang No, Sally wasn't the last person to see Bella alive.

May What?

Mrs Lang That was Emily. She was the last person to see Bella alive — and the first person to find her dead. That could look bad too — couldn't it?

May What are you suggesting?

Mrs Lang Sometimes I hardly dare suggest to myself. But it's been on my mind. We'll never really know what happened that night. And now I don't want to. There were bruises. Something may have happened that finally unbalanced Emily. They may have quarrelled.

May Why should they? Emily was fond of Bella.

Mrs Lang No, it was more that she needed her. Ever since her husband died Emily's been looking for a rock to cling to. She made Bella that rock. And when that rock began to crumble ... I never gave any of this much thought until you said she could walk ...

They both glance at the bathroom door

May But, Diana, suppose she's made me her rock — suppose she wanted to cling to me? Suppose she thinks I'm crumbling?

Mrs Lang I don't think that's anything for you to worry about. The obsession's with Bella — not with you.

May I'm not so sure. I know this may sound silly but I can't find my hatpin. And I think she's got it.

Mrs Lang (*smiling*) May, I have to say — that does sound silly. You probably lost it out there in the dark.

May That's what Emily said but there was something in the way she said it.
  I didn't believe her. Why should I believe her? Didn't you say she was
  mad?

Mrs Lang May, calm down. She won't be any trouble tonight. I've increased
  the strength of her tablets. It's not ethical — I should inform her but under
  the circumstances ... She'll sleep like a baby.

May I shan't. I shan't close my eyes.

Mrs Lang You'd better have a couple as well. (*She places some tablets by
  May's bed*) In the morning I'll see if I can separate you. This really isn't
  working.

May You'll move me out?

Mrs Lang No, I think this may be the time to move Emily to somewhere a
  little more secure ...

*There are sounds from the bathroom. Mrs Lang puts a finger to her lips. She
crosses and opens the bathroom door*

  Come along, Emily, my dear. You're palely loitering ... Time to hit the
  hay...

Emily (*off*) Who's that?

Mrs Lang Your lady of the bedchamber.

  Mrs Lang assists Emily out of the bathroom

*During the following Mrs Lang assists Emily into bed, leaving her dressing-
gown draped on the bedcover. May picks up her tablets and hides them under
her pillow*

Emily Don't pull me.

Mrs Lang I'm not pulling you.

Emily Don't shove.

Mrs Lang I'm not shoving you, Emily, dear. I'm making you comfortable.

Emily I've never been comfortable since I've been here.

Mrs Lang (*sighing*) Neither have we, Emily.

Mrs Lang makes Emily comfortable

  Now, take your tablets.

Emily peers at the tablets

Emily These aren't the right ones — these are different.

Mrs Lang They are the ones — they're just a different shape, that's all.

Emily I'll never swallow these.

Mrs Lang Of course you will.
Emily They'll stick in my throat.
Mrs Lang Now, down the hatch.

Emily swallows the tablets

There that wasn't too bad, was it? And if you need anything, Emily, don't disturb May — ring for Sally. That's what she's there for. (*She pauses by the door and switches off the main light, winking at May as she does so*)

Emily removes the tablets from her mouth and slips them into her dressing-gown pocket

Night, girls.

Mrs Lang exits

Emily What was that wink for?
May She didn't wink.
Emily She did. And what were you talking about while I was in there?
May Nothing.
Emily It sounded like a lot of nothing to me. You're getting very cosy again you two. (*She studies May*) She did put you here, didn't she?
May Of course she put me here — you don't think I came from choice, do you?
Emily You know what I mean. You were put here to report back.
May Of course not.
Emily You think you're so clever but you don't know what you're getting involved in. It's a conspiracy — they're all in it. Vernon Watts. Sally. Mrs Lang. The doctor.
May (*gaping*) The doctor! How did he get involved?
Emily He signs the death certificates — probably helps out with the odd lethal injection as well. He's putty in her hands. I've seen her rubbing against him. They work together: Vernon Watts charms them, finds out about money — Sally finishes them off. And Lang takes care of the paperwork.

May's mouth drops open even further

May My God! They're right about you. You're mad.
Emily We'll see if I'm mad. In the meantime I'm not waking up tomorrow with my throat cut. Drop the catch on the door.
May (*appalled*) I can't. That lock was put on for the staff. We're not supposed to use it.

Emily If they can lock the door so can we. Tomorrow we'll discharge ourselves and book into a hotel.

May No!

Emily Why not? It couldn't be any more expensive than this place. We could have afternoon tea in the lounge — cocktails before dinner.

May Emily, I'm not booking into a hotel with you — and I'm not locking myself in with you either.

Emily gives May a grim smile

Emily What's the matter? Are you frightened?

May No ...

Emily Does this remind you of one of those films ...?

May What films?

Emily Where an old lady with a heart problem goes round bolting the doors and window to keep the murderer out only to find ...

May What?

Emily That she's locked the murderer in with her.

May Emily, now you are frightening me.

Emily That's what you all think, isn't it? That I did it.

May No.

Emily Then lock that door.

May No, I'm going to get ready for bed.

May exits into the bathroom

Emily hesitates and then drags herself out of bed

Emily You're a fool, May Brewer. (*During the following she limps to the door and quietly drops the catch*) You're not in the film with the lady who has a heart problem. You're in this film where a crippled, lonely old lady is being pursued by a homicidal maniac but no-one believes her because she's old — not even her best friend. And they all want to put her in the booby hatch. (*She returns to bed*)

May emerges angrily from the bathroom

May Emily, I'm not your best friend.

Emily Not any more you're not.

May And you're not crippled.

Emily Is that what you told her?

May hesitates and is about to speak when someone tries the outer door. May freezes. The door is rattled for a moment and then there is silence

May That was someone trying the door. You've locked it!
Emily It's all right — they've gone away.
May There'll be ructions in the morning. (*She heads for the door*)
Emily (*sharply*) Leave it.

May hesitates

May If you can't walk — how did you drop that catch?
Emily I have my good days.
May (*defiantly*) And did you have a good day — the day Bella died?
Emily What do you mean? Come on — spit it out. I know it's choking you.
(*She leans back wearily on her pillows*)

May sits on her bed. She can't see Emily

May I know a worse film than those two.
Emily What's that?
May Where someone's been taken over.
Emily Taken over?
May By alien beings. They come from outer space and they're so ugly we
couldn't stand the sight of them — so they take human form. They could
even be a member of your own family — even a close personal friend. The
only difference is they have a stud in the back of their neck ——

Emily closes her eyes wearily

— and that's how they're controlled — how they get their messages. And
if they play up they get a shock through it. Oh, and their little fingers stick
out; I don't know why that is but you only notice it when they're shaking
hands or drinking tea — things like that. They're the only ways you can tell
them apart. In every other way they look and act just like anyone else.
(*Pause*) Except they have a monotonous way of speaking and this faraway
look in their eyes — as if they're only half awake. But you don't always
notice that — you certainly wouldn't around here … (*She waits for a
response from Emily*)

But Emily's eyes are closed and she's breathing regularly

I suppose that's what murderers are like. Like alien beings. They go around
looking just like you and me. Only they don't have studs in their necks and
their little fingers don't stick out, so you can't tell them apart. And they're
not controlled and they know what they're doing. But underneath they're
ugly — so ugly we couldn't stand the sight of them. I don't suppose they
could even stand the sight of themselves — that's why they try to look like

the rest of us. And they have no feelings because they're aliens. They can't feel what we feel. God hasn't given them that. (*Pause*) That's why I don't want that door locked, Emily. I've been afraid ever since I knew you could walk. Afraid to close my eyes. You were alone with Bella that night. What happened? (*Pause*) Emily?

May moves around the corner and sees that Emily is asleep. She tip-toes across to the bed. She picks up Emily's dressing-gown which is draped across the bed and searches the pockets for the hatpin. She frowns and produces the tablets Emily was supposed to have swallowed and looks at them in consternation

Emily shoots out a hand and grabs May

Emily What do you think you're doing?
May I was going to hang up your dressing-gown.
Emily Leave it. It's perishing in here.
May You didn't take your tablets.
Emily (*grinning*) No. They weren't the right ones.
May (*defiantly*) Neither were mine. (*She pulls away*)
Emily Then should we get some sleep — the hard way? Unless you're afraid of alien beings … (*She releases her grip*)
May (*bravely*) I'm not afraid.

Emily switches off her lamp. The only light now comes from May's bedside lamp

You're right — the room is cold. I'm going to bed. (*She removes her slippers, sits and puts her hands together. Softly*) Yea, though I walk through the valley of the shadow of death, I will fear no evil: for thou art with me; thy rod and thy staff comfort me … (*She hesitates and then takes a stiff drink of sherry. She switches off her lamp*)

The room is now in total darkness

Emily's breathing becomes more regular — almost a snore

I hope you're not going to snore.

The breathing becomes mingled with a different sound, the sound of the breeze outside

I wish I could get warm. There'll be trouble in the morning over that door. Well, I'm not taking responsibility … Emily? (*Nervously*) Emily, is that you? (*Her voice breaks off*)

Mrs Lang enters (unseen in the darkness) via the emergency door and moves DL of May's bed

Emily (unseen in the darkness) gets out of bed and stands DR of May's bed

In the darkness there's a gasp and the sound of a faint struggle. The sound of the breeze grows louder and so do the gasps for breath. There is a long, loud scream from Mrs Lang

May's bedside light is switched on. May is leaning back on her pillows. She has one hand to her throat and the other is clutching the table lamp. She is struggling for breath. Emily, on the DR side of the bed, is supporting herself against the wall. Mrs Lang, on the opposite side, looks pale and angry. She is clutching her shoulder from which the hatpin protrudes; blood oozes through her fingers. Her face is contorted in pain. She pulls the hatpin from her shoulder and more blood follows

Mrs Lang You insane creature! Look what you've done. (*At the sight of her blood she falters and sits on the bed*)

Sally hurries into the room

Late again, Sally.
Sally I came as soon as I could.
Mrs Lang It would have been too late. I asked you to be vigilant. I warned you about Mrs Baines' mental state.
Emily (*wearily*) I'm not in a mental state.

Mrs Lang's tone changes

Mrs Lang Of course you are, dear. And it's worse at night. That's why you need to be watched. (*To Sally*) I was only just in time. I found them struggling.
Emily We weren't struggling.
Mrs Lang You were. But perhaps you've already forgotten. Sally, help Emily to a chair.

Sally takes Emily's arm and assists her to her chair

(*Eyeing Emily sardonically*) So you can walk, Emily. (*To Sally*) Are we witnessing a miracle, or is this evidence of a deviousness we so often come across in these cases …
Emily Who's a case? I'm not a case.
Mrs Lang No, of course not. Sally, get me a towel. (*She glances at Emily*) I think she's over the worst.

Sally fetches a towel from the bathroom

Mrs Lang removes her coat

May is struggling to regain her breath

Poor May. I'm neglecting you. How do you feel?
May I felt this pillow over my face. I couldn't breathe.

Sally looks at May over Mrs Lang's shoulder

Sally She's in shock.
Mrs Lang You'll feel better soon.

Mrs Lang pours May a glass of sherry and helps her to drink it

(*Rapidly*) It's all my fault. I shouldn't have left them together. May tried
to warn me. It's not even poor Emily's fault. She can't help herself. The
fault was mine. I should have read the signs. You'd better ring the doctor,
Sally — the emergency number. She'll need to be sedated and put in the
secure wing. Tomorrow I'll ring Green Acres and speak to the resident
psychiatrist. She needs help, poor thing. (*Pause*) Can you manage her? She
may need restraining.

*Sally takes Emily's arm. They look at each other. Sally sees something in
Emily's eyes she hasn't seen before — fear, panic, a struggle for self-control.
Sally's customary hard expression changes*

Sally (*quietly*) I don't think she needs restraining.
Emily Let me sit for a minute.

Sally releases Emily's arm

Mrs Lang exits into the bathroom dabbing at the wound on her arm

So that's how she did it.
Sally What?
Emily Can you feel how cold the room is? It was like that the night Bella died.
It wasn't the prowler who came that night. It was her. Through that door.
(*She points to the door leading to the fire escape*) She must have taken
Vernon's key from him. She had Bella's money. Bella was going to tell
Vernon. Lang couldn't have that. It would have meant prison. So she killed
her. And she's been trying to put the blame on everyone else ever since.
And I was helping her. Then I became a fly in the ointment. She thought

I knew something. And she couldn't find that bank statement. She wanted to know what I was up to. That's why she put May in here. But May was getting curious. And although no-one would listen to me they might listen to May. But then May was known to have a weak heart ...

Mrs Lang appears silently from the bathroom and watches Emily

If May died there'd be no questions asked and if they did ask questions — what would they have thought? Locked in here with a mad old lady — just the two of them — and the old lady fit to be tied — an old lady who'd done it before.

Mrs Lang Did you do it before, Emily?

Emily (*staring*) What?

Mrs Lang Isn't that what you're saying, my dear? That you've done it before? That is what you're saying isn't it?

Emily tries to focus

Emily No. I didn't mean ...

Mrs Lang Better take her downstairs, Sally — and be gentle with her ... (*She opens the door*)

Alan is standing in the threshold

(*Staring in surprise*) Mr Baines! What are you doing here?

Sally I rang him.

Mrs Lang Whatever for?

Alan I asked Sally to ring if she was concerned about my mother.

Mrs Lang Sally, I've told you before, we don't involve outsiders in our problems.

Sally I couldn't find you. I thought Mr Baines should know. I thought I was using my initiative.

Mrs Lang Well, it can't be helped — it's done now.

Alan And after all, I'm hardly an outsider. Emily is my mother.

Mrs Lang (*coldly*) Oh, you've remembered that, have you?

Alan Yes. And if there's cause for concern ...

Mrs Lang You could say that. Since you're here you may as well know. I came up here to find your mother struggling in the dark with May — she had a pillow over her face — and in the resulting struggle she stabbed me with a hatpin. Satisfied?

Alan (*staring*) Did you do all that? Mother?

Emily (*quietly*) No. Not that you'll believe me.

Mrs Lang Don't worry, Mr Baines — I shan't bring charges. Your mother can't help herself — but she must be put somewhere safe, where she can be properly examined. For her own sake — and for the sake of the rest of us. After all, this is supposed to be a rest home — and we've been getting precious little rest since your mother arrived.

Alan remains staring down at Emily

(*Smiling*) I imagine now you wish you'd stayed at home and finished that pizza.

Alan But why did she stab you?

Mrs Lang Mr Baines, you haven't been listening.

Alan But I have, Mrs Lang — at the door. My mother seems to think May was in danger from you.

Mrs Lang May, would you tell Mr Baines what happened? He doesn't seem to think his mother is capable of violence.

May My brain's a whirl. All I know is there was a pillow over my face and someone was trying to kill me.

Alan But not necessarily my mother.

Mrs Lang Isn't that taking family loyalty a little far, Mr Baines?

Alan I'm merely pointing out it's one word against another.

Mrs Lang One word against another! The word of a matron against that of a lunatic old woman? (*She stops, aware of the effect of those words*) Not that we use those words here ...

Emily Ask her for Bella's bank statement.

Alan Is there a statement?

Mrs Lang I've no idea what she's talking about — I'm afraid she's wandering.

May There is a statement — I've seen it.

Mrs Lang I'm afraid you're confused, May.

Alan So am I. Perhaps I could see these papers, Mrs Lang? Put our minds at rest.

Mrs Lang What?

Alan Should we go down to your office? I could go through the papers while you get your arm fixed.

Mrs Lang Look through my papers? Mr Baines, you're beginning to sound like a policeman.

Alan Mrs Lang, I am a policeman. (*He produces his warrant card*)

Mrs Lang What! But you never said. Your mother never mentioned it.

Alan (*smiling*) No — it's one of the many secrets I'm forced to share with my mother. She doesn't like me to tell people. She says it makes them uncomfortable. Do I make you feel uncomfortable, Mrs Lang?

Mrs Lang Certainly not. Since you're prepared to listen to your mother's ramblings — perhaps you'd like to have her back?

Alan (*uneasily*) What?

Mrs Lang You wouldn't like that, would you? They're all dumped here like garbage: all they carry is a suitcase, all they hear is the roar of a departing car — and the rest is silence. And we have to keep that garbage tidy, and clean, and contented. Let me ask you something. Would you have her back?

Alan remains silent

Of course you wouldn't. You don't want the mess — you leave that for us to tidy up. I'm afraid this concern for your mother comes a little late.

Alan Don't talk about her as if she's not here. She's still an individual.

Mrs Lang She was once but her clock stopped a long time ago — just like the one on the dresser. And you know that as well as I do.

Alan That may be true. But even a stopped clock tells the right time twice a day, Mrs Lang. Down to the thousandth of a second. Who's to say this isn't the time? Now, I want to see those papers. If you have a problem with that — I can get a warrant. I can also take my mother away from here. And, incidentally, I don't see her as garbage.

Mrs Lang (*hastily*) I didn't mean that. I ——

Alan Then what did you mean? Perhaps you saw Bella Bottomley as garbage?

Mrs Lang No!

Alan To be disposed of?

Mrs Lang You're being preposterous.

Alan You said there were bruises.

Mrs Lang They had nothing to do with me.

Alan You're the matron. What happens here has everything to do with you. Did you receive any money from Bella Bottomley?

Mrs Lang What?

Alan Did you, Mrs Lang?

Mrs Lang (*after a hesitation*) Well, there were certain donations — to the Amenity Fund — to members of staff ...

Alan And were you included in these donations?

Mrs Lang (*after a pause*) Well, yes ...

Alan Were they substantial?

Mrs Lang Bella was very grateful for the treatment she received here — very grateful.

Alan (*gesturing towards the door*) Should we look at these — donations?

Mrs Lang (*defiantly*) Certainly. I have nothing to hide. (*She turns to leave*)

Alan One more question, Mrs Lang. How did you get here?

Mrs Lang (*staring*) Get here? I was leaving. I'd even said good-night to Sally. Then I realized I hadn't checked on Mrs James. Whilst I was in there

I heard noises from up here. I remembered May's fears for her safety and came straight up. You know what I found?

Alan I know what you said you found but what you should have found was a locked door.

Mrs Lang (*astonished*) What?

Alan This door was locked, Mrs Lang.

Mrs Lang That door's never locked.

Alan It was tonight. That's why Sally sent for me.

Sally That's what kept me. I was looking for the key. (*She holds out the key*)

Mrs Lang stares uncomprehendingly at the key

Alan So you see — you couldn't have come through that door ... (*He moves to the emergency door*) No. The door you came through was this one. (*He opens the emergency door*) The same door you came through the night Bella Bottomley died. (*He takes Mrs Lang gently by the arm*) Perhaps we could talk about that as well.

For the first time Mrs Lang loses her composure and chokes back a sob

Mrs Lang backs out of the room followed by Alan

Sally (*moving around the room excitedly*) Will you two be all right? I don't want to miss this.

Sally exits without waiting for a reply

Emily and May look at each other in silence for a moment

May Well, that's put the cat amongst the pigeons.

Emily No thanks to you. You were a washout. "My brain's in a whirl." You almost had me in a padded cell.

May It was your fault. You had me suspecting everyone. (*Pause*) I must say, Emily, for someone with bad legs you can move fast enough when you want to.

Emily I have my good days. Besides, that was nervous energy. I was galvanized by fear.

May I was frozen with fear.

Emily Were you? Well, I must say for someone with a weak heart you stood up to the ordeal very well. I know people with strong hearts that wouldn't have come through that.

May I wonder what my last words would have been.

Emily "Get that pillow off my face", I should think.

They giggle

I'm getting hysterical.
May So am I. (*Pause*) You never told me your Alan was a policeman.
Emily You never asked.
May Would you have told me?
Emily No.

They giggle again

May I suppose we'll have to give some evidence.
Emily Of course. All eyes will be upon us, May. They'll have to listen to us for a change. The judge will probably allow me to give evidence from the well of the court.
May (*slyly*) Unless it's one of your good days ... I wonder what I'll say?
Emily The usual. "My brain was in a whirl."
May Emily, why did you pretend you couldn't walk? Was it for the disability?
Emily (*indignantly*) No! (*Pause*) It was for the same reason you make out you've got a weak heart. I was looking for some tender loving care. I didn't get it so I did it more and more. I still didn't get it — by then it was too late to change.
May I haven't had any tender loving care since Harry died. And Frank never comes. I think he's ashamed of me. Funny how things change. I used to shush him as a boy — now he shushes me.
Emily I know. I was always telling Alan to eat his greens, now he tells me to eat mine. He says I haven't got any trace elements. Whatever they are.
May Still, he stood up for you tonight.
Emily That was in his professional capacity. He'd have arrested me if it had been necessary. (*Pause*) Do you know what he accused me of tonight? Shoving soap up his backside.
May Whatever for?
Emily Constipation. It was a sovereign remedy.
May I didn't know that.
Emily Oh, yes.
May (*after a pause*) They weren't big pieces, were they?
Emily Of course not. It's thanks to me he's not constipated today. Well, if he is — he never mentions it.
May I'm not surprised.
Emily You do your best, but it's never good enough. We've lived too long, May — that's our trouble.
May I know I've lived a long time, Emily, and I feel old but I've never felt — mature.

Emily No-one ever does, if you ask me.

May I wonder if I should ring Frank and tell him about this?

Emily Why not? (*Pause*) Why don't you tell him about Walter as well?

May No. I couldn't, Emily. It would be too much of a shock.

Emily Perhaps he could do with a shock.

May They say that revelation late in life could cause nervous breakdown.

Emily Well, if anyone could be improved by a nervous breakdown, it's your Frank.

May Emily!

Emily He could take you to see the grave.

May Walter's?

Emily Yes.

May In Holland?

Emily It would be an outing. They keep them immaculate. Very tidy people, the Dutch.

May I've always wanted to …

Emily Well, don't leave it too late.

May (*after a pause*) Emily, if you were me, would you tell Frank?

Emily No.

May Well I'm blessed! But you expect me to.

Emily We're not the same, May. If we were plants you'd be a flower and I'd be a berry. Berries don't open — they don't have to. But if a flower doesn't open it dies.

May Perhaps I'll ring him in the morning. I'm tired.

Emily I'm cold. Check to see if he closed that door.

May sighs, gets out of bed and checks the glass door

May It's closed but it's not locked.

Emily So there's nothing to stop Vernon Watts coming in here and having his wicked way with you.

May (*giggling*) Emily.

Emily leans back on her pillow

Emily Well, at least we'll be able to get out if there's a fire — that's one consolation. We won't be burnt to a crisp.

May There's no danger of that. There are safeguards.

Emily What safeguards?

May There are sprinklers.

Emily What?

May Sprinklers — in the ceiling.

Emily (*after a pause*) I wish you hadn't said that.

May What?
Emily Sprinklers. I shall have to go.
May Oh, no.

Emily struggles out of bed

Emily Give me a hand.
May Ring the bell.
Emily I'm not ringing the bell tonight.
May Well, can't you manage?
Emily After what I've been through?

May sighs and assists Emily towards the bathroom

   Don't pull me.
May I'm not pulling.
Emily And don't shove.
May I'm not shoving. I'm just wondering what your last servant died of.

Emily stops for a moment and looks at May

Emily She was murdered — but no-one listened ...

The Lights fade to Black-out

CURTAIN

FURNITURE AND PROPERTY LIST

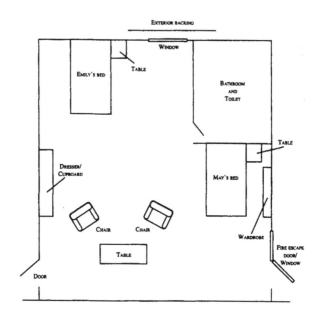

EXTERIOR BACKING

WINDOW

TABLE

EMILY'S BED

BATHROOM
AND
TOILET

TABLE

DRESSER/
CUPBOARD

MAY'S BED

CHAIR   CHAIR

WARDROBE

FIRE ESCAPE
DOOR/
WINDOW

TABLE

DOOR

ACT I
SCENE 1

On stage: Two single beds
Two bell cords
Two bedside tables with drawers. *On both*: practical lamps and
   decanters of water. *On **Emily**'s*: music box containing cupboard
   key. *On **May**'s*: handbag containing bottle of scent. *In the drawer
   of **May**'s*: bottle of sherry, purse, prayerbook, brooch
Wardrobe. *In it*: **May**'s hat and hatpin
Two easy chairs with cushions
Occasional table. *On it*: tea things
Large old-fashioned dresser/cupboard covered in bric-a-brac. *In it*:
   presentation clock with piece of paper in the back; blue purse
   containing tissue paper, small scissors, cotton wool, opal ring,
   crucifix, sapphire ring
Wheelchair
Local paper for **May**

Furniture and Property List   61

Off stage: Tray (**Sally**)
                Tray of tea things (**Mrs Lang**)

Personal: **Sally**: list

<h2 style="text-align:center">SCENE 2</h2>

Re-set: Blue purse and contents, wheelchair for **Emily**, window curtains open

Set: Tinsel and holly

Off stage: Two glasses (**Mrs Lang**)

ACT II

Set: Glass of sherry for **May**

Off stage: Bottle of eyedrops (**Sally**)
                Key (**Sally**)
                Towel (**Sally**)

Personal: **Mrs Lang**: bottle of tablets; later, replica of hatpin protruding from
                shoulder with "blood"

LIGHTING PLOT

Practical fittings required: two bedside lamps
One interior. The same throughout

ACT I, Scene 1

To open: General interior lighting

No cues

ACT I, Scene 2

To open: General interior lighting

No cues

ACT II

To open: General interior lighting; practicals on

Cue 1	**Mrs Lang** switches off the main light *Cut general interior lighting*	(Page 47)
Cue 2	**Emily** switches off her lamp *Snap off* **Emily**'s *lamp*	(Page 50)
Cue 3	**May** switches off her lamp *Snap off* **May**'s *lamp*	(Page 50)
Cue 4	**May** switches on her lamp *Snap on* **May**'s *lamp*	(Page 51)
Cue 5	**Emily**: " ... but no-one listened ..." *Fade to black-out*	(Page 59)

EFFECTS PLOT

ACT I

Cue 1   **Alan** lifts the lid of the music box   (Page 16)
Music; cut when lid closed

Cue 2   **Alan**: "Because you won't try."   (Page 30)
Sound of departing coach

ACT II

Cue 3   **May** opens the music box   (Page 43)
Music; cut when lid closed

Cue 4   **May**: "I hope you're not going to snore."   (Page 50)
Sound of breeze outside

Cue 5   Gasp and faint struggle   (Page 51)
Increase sound of breeze